Vignettes in Verse

By
Kristina Kearns

Dedicated to My Angel

Anita

To touch your heart,
make you smile,
or give you food for
thought.

Krestina Kearns

Anita

Gingerly I left my bed
And hobbled down the hall
Where cradled babies lay in wait
To pay their moms a call

I looked and looked to find my child
And there she was at last
My darling precious baby
In beauty she was cast

I should have known right from the start
This child was like no other
With fire in determined eyes
And awesome to her mother

Beauty, brains and talent
A heart and soul to sing
A free and lilting spirit
Yearning to take wing

A symphony of love rings out
From Karen, Beth and Gail
Echoes from her sisters
Will evermore prevail

Rich in family, rich in friends
And fierce in loyalty
But most of all for Sean and John
Her love eternally

Through life's joys and sorrows
Beyond the grief and strife
Remembering my darling
I'll celebrate her life

Mom
*

Table of Contents

Memoir

A Love Story
(My Mom and Dad)

When dad was in his nineties enrapt in memory
He spoke of when he first saw mom and uttered, "That's for me"

She was but a teen from a little mining town
Checking hats and coats in a nightclub of renown

Dad was in his tux on the bandstand with his horn
Doing what he loved—for music he was born

That's how it all began oh so long ago
Seeds of love were sown and time would see them grow

It wasn't always easy—dad would ride the bus
With gigs across the land while mom was home with us

I remember mama with tears in her eyes
Dad was having fun—he didn't realize

Years rolled by in cadence—mom began to fail
Dad's love for her had blossomed—devotion would prevail

I overheard my mom one night calling out his name
"I will care for you my love," softly he'd proclaim

Tears filled my eyes as I listened in the dark
The depth of their love forever made its mark

'Whispering'—an oldie—'while you cuddle near'
A song they called their own—their voices, I still hear

*

My Father

Music was his life
From when he was a boy
Reaching deep within his soul
It was his greatest joy

So many in his family
Had music to impart
A wondrous gift bestowed on him
A song within his heart

He became a Rhythm King
When he was just a teen
The tempo reigned at twilight
And all the years between

Night clubs, cruises, one night gigs
Rippling rhythm rings
In good times and depression
Lilting music springs

The best thing ever in his life
His daughters heard him say
Was when he met their mother
His true love come what may

And now the song grows distant
Echoing above
Ringing out his legacy
His melody of love

*

My Mother

Born in Pennsylvania
In a little mining town
The first of many children
Siblings all around

Her father came from far away
He sailed across the sea
He wed his fair haired maiden
And raised a family

The home was filled with discipline
With rules ordained by God
The culture of the day declared
"Do not spare the rod"

The eldest of the children
Her treatment most severe
Still, she kept a loving heart
Her parents, she held dear

Gentleness and love she gave
To sister and to me
And kindness flowed to animals
A kitten brought her glee

She was a pretty lady
She caught my father's eye
Now sweet memories remain
Of my mother's lullaby

*

My Sister

On a special day in my life at the age of two
My parents gave a gift to me to last my whole life through

Behold my baby sister—cute as she could be
My first little playmate for all the world to see

When we were very little and got into a fight
Our mother in her wisdom always made things right

Across the floor she'd draw an imaginary line
And place us face to face—I remember auld lang syne

"Now, kiss and make up," mother dear would say
"Beneath a different roof you each will live one day"

And so our mom proved right—the years took us apart
But only in proximity—not within the heart

Bonds of love would grow as time consumed the years
Echoing sweet tenderness in laughter and through tears

Thank heaven for that blessed day and the gift bestowed on me
Loving sister—dearest friend—that's what she'll always be

*

Early Memory

My mother pushed the carriage that held my sister and me
On a pleasant summer eve—a vision I still see

Flares from Coney Island filled a starry night
Fireworks exploding brought baby sister fright

She was just a little one and began to cry
My mother took her in her arms—her tears she wished to dry

Every Tuesday evening the fireworks display
Brought the children running with a hoot and a loud hooray

As we grew each summer, we came to join the crowd
Amid the cheering children, we were just as loud

My sister came to savor the fireworks brigade
We'd run with all the others and she was not afraid

I still can see my mother—oh so long ago
A young and lively presence, with love she watched us grow

I still can see my sister when I was barely three
A sweet and fragile baby in a loving memory

*

My Old Neighborhood

We walked to Coney Island—it wasn't very far
Or we took a noisy ride on a trolley car

The screeching and the clanging, we never heard at all
It only cost a nickel when we were very small

An ethnic city neighborhood where dark haired children played
Two towheads, the exception, I and sister made

My mother was a green eyed blond, my father tall and dark
We spoke a kind of English with a New York City spark

I was a little tomboy and telephone poles I'd climb
Trees were not abundant, but I had a grand old time

We played a captive kind of game called Ringaleevio
Held till someone tagged you, then you were free to go

City kids played stoop ball—they know what I mean
If you hit the pointed edge—you would score fifteen

Seasons were not visual with concrete all aglow
In summer ocean breezes, in winter sometimes snow

Depression passed and then came war, such changes as we grew
The older boys went off to fight—the big one—World War II

Some things I remember well of my old neighborhood
Where I would love to walk once more—if I only could

*

School Days

Deep within my memory rests my first day of school
My mother brought me to the class—I thought I was so cool

I remember thinking that I was really brave
There were children crying, while trying to behave

Reading, writing, 'rithmetic, and so much more to learn
As time marched on in cadence, a page in life would turn

I recall my recitation of the Gettysburg Address
In the school assembly—I tried hard to impress

My teacher did some coaching, "Pause before the crowd
Wait before you start to speak—make your teacher proud"

I walked across the stage—what would be my stance?
A pause, and then a hiking of my drooping underpants

And here's another memory—our teacher said, "don't speak"
We were in a fire drill and her words were not in Greek

But then I saw my sister—I forgot and I called out
The teacher was upon me and slapped my head about

Memories to cherish—some best to forget
Nostalgia of my long ago remains with me yet

Soon the sands of time would softly fall away
And take my childhood with it forever come what may

*

My Cousin

Memories of childhood
Take us far away
Memories of loving bonds
Still holding fast today

We grew up side by side
Her house was next to mine
We caused a little mischief
But rarely crossed the line

Except one day so long ago
Together time was spent
Up on grandpa's work of art
The day we broke his tent

No longer are we neighbors
A rendezvous we seek
She wears a white carnation
Of course with tongue in cheek

She is a lifelong treasure
Buddies to the end
My father's sister's daughter
Loving cousin, friend

*

My Shiny Bicycle

A row of shiny bicycles
Stood before my eyes
"Pick one out," daddy said
Much to my surprise

My often absent father
Bought a gift for me
A sweet attempt to show his love
It was plain to see

I rode my shiny bicycle
Around the neighborhood
Knowing daddy loved me
Made me feel so good

And now I ride my bicycle
Round and round again
I think about that happy day
That happy day back when

*

Calvin

Up before the rooster crowed
When he was just a lad
Hard work was his daily grind
Ordered by his dad

Work from dawn to sunset
Endless chores all day
He grew up on a dairy farm
Where toil pre-empted play

My mother's kin were neighbors
That's how I came to meet
The man, when I was very young
Who'd sweep me off my feet

His charm was overwhelming
With a twinkle in his eye
His sense of humor echoing
He made me smile and sigh

This was the beginning
It was plain to see
He'd be there to help me
Raise a family

He was a man of faith and love
And steadfast in his creed
He dwells within my yesterday
And in my heart indeed

*

A Mother's Love

On a special day in my life
A day like no other
I recall—I said aloud
"Today you are a mother"

A feeling swelled within my heart
Of that there is no doubt
An overwhelming feeling
Of what love is all about

This newborn babe and those to come
Made me realize
A mother's love is boundless
It opened up my eyes

It made me think of my own mom
And what she felt for me
Of little things she told me
When she held me on her knee

Now we've come full circle
Many years have flown
My babies know this feeling
With babies of their own

*

My Babies

Gail

There is nothing like it—the magic of firstborn
She came to me in my youth and brightened up each morn

From clinging little baby, she branched out on her own
And now an individual with ideas hers alone

She has a sense of humor—she's special in her ways
A little girl with many friends from kindergarten days

As time goes by in countless ways, she means so much to me
No matter who came after, the first she'll always be

***

Anita

Gingerly I left my bed and hobbled down the hall
Where cradled babies lay in wait to pay their moms a call

I looked and looked to find my child and there she was at last
My darling precious baby, in beauty she was cast

I should have known right from the start this child was like no other
With fire in determined eyes and awesome to her mother

Beauty brains and talent, a heart and soul to sing
A free and lilting spirit yearning to take wing

Through life's joys and sorrows beyond the grief and strife
Remembering my darling I'll celebrate her life

***

Karen

A special place in my heart this child of mine holds fast
With memories deep within of magic moments past

One Halloween so long ago, we two embraced the road
Mid gremlins, ghosts, and goblins and swirling leaves, we strode

And then our Christmas moment with magic in the air
Together when we saw the lights—a colored brilliant glare

She has a love of learning so beautiful to see
She speaks of it with glowing eyes and sensitivity

To make a difference in young lives is her lofty goal
She gives it everything she has from her heart and soul

***

Elisabeth

The baby of the family—the apple of our eye
She'll always be my Betsy as years march quickly by

When she was just a little girl and time with her we'd spend
She'd talk of Laurie Thinton, her imaginary friend

And with a visit to a zoo with animals so great
Only to the kitty cats would she gravitate

And now a grown-up lady with changes through the years
But still the apple of my eye and music to my ears

***

My Grandchildren

Jody Ann

Jody is my princess—I think of her and smile
She is the first, my only girl—she's regal and has style
A girl in quest of noble dreams with lofty peaks to climb
I'm proud of all that she's become—a woman of her time
***

Sean

When I recall a little boy my heart proudly sings
I see him still, telling me of dinosaurs and things
Echoes of his love of lore fill his resume
I revel in the joy of him for the man he is today
***

Todd

A partnership of school and work rings out loud and clear
Ambition is a theme for him in quest of his career
A sense of humor serves him well with a chuckle here and there
He warms my heart in many ways—a lad beyond compare
***

Mitchell

Once he was my littlest boy but now he's quite a man
With focus on attire he's the dandy in our clan
A man of many talents he holds sway in art
He holds a very special place in the corner of my heart
***

John-Henri

John-Henri is a special guy—he is the youngest one
Artistic like his mom is he—he is his mother's son
Though he's quite the joker with messages and things
His music reaches in my heart and for him my love springs
***

*

A Message to My Grandchildren

Things that I have learned / Lo these many years
I share with you my darlings / My precious ones—my dears

A heart that's light in spirit / Where hurt feelings melt away
Will bloom in sweet serenity / More than words can say

Hard work may seem daunting / And may not be much fun
But the nicest kind of 'tired' / Is from a job well done

A promise is a sacred vow / One's word is cast in stone
Something to remember / Your name is yours alone

It matters not what happens / When we're down and out
It's how we face the challenge / That's what it's all about

All things pass with time / Sunshine follows rain
In trying times remember / There's joy beyond the pain

America the beautiful / How fortunate we are
The greatest nation, we call home / O thank that lucky star

Take note of golden moments / Smell the fragrant flowers
Hold them in your heart / Treasure sunshine hours

*

Joey
(My Beloved Nephew)

He played many roles in life
A soul of style and grace
Husband, father, brother, son
He walked in love's embrace

To Jerry and Anita
He was their only boy
With every step along the way
He was their pride and joy

To Vicki, Lisa, Eve his twin
Sibling love so pure
Golden places in their hearts
Will evermore endure

Brilliant color glistens
In the portrait of his life
He found his love, sweet Sara
His everything, his wife

Together they would face the world
With dreams that touch the sky
Along came joy—Alyssa
The apple of their eye

And now we celebrate his life
A tale of honor bright
We cherish all our memories
Of his shining light

*

Festival Choir

Once upon a time there lived a joyous choir
That echoed far and wide with spirit, soul and fire

Cathedral walls resounded when sweet music filled the air
And the bishop draped in splendor raised his voice in prayer

Beloved maestro Joe in his own delightful way
Brought forth lilting rhapsody with each cantabile

The congregation reveled in the beauty of the sound
They stood in grand applause and it rippled all around

For many, many years the choir sang with soul
With music from their hearts—this was their noble goal

And then with little warning change was in the air
The choir was dismantled mid sadness and despair

No more fond rehearsals—no more sweet cantata
No more choir family for persona non grata

A hole was left within the heart—what was there to do
Time to move along and look for something new

*

School Again

A sweet reward in life has been
To raise my family
My babies brought me so much joy
A priceless memory

But time had come for something new
My children were all grown
Caring for each one of them
Was all I'd ever known

Back to school—a dream of mine
That was the thing for me
A chance for learning and for growth
And vast discovery

I forced myself to venture forth
Filled with doubt and fear
Walking down the halls I thought
"What am I doing here?"

I grit my teeth and stuck it out
Through wind and snow and rain
And then to my delight I found
I had a working brain

Knowledge gained and people met
Adorn my every day
Like ever growing flowers
In a blossoming bouquet

*

Bill

An isle of melancholy
And tenderness is he
An isle of deep reflection
Resourceful as can be

With boy-like fascination
Of soldiers, guns and ships
Of history locked in yesterday
Antiquity he grips

In search of life's amenities
Upon the door he knocks
And he likes the ladies
And scotch upon the rocks

A love of life, its joy, its pang
And festive revelry
There is music in his soul
A poignant melody

To me he is Sir William
High up on a hill
With vice and virtue rolled in one
To me he is my Bill

Our lives embrace each other
Forever come what may
We step forward hand in hand
To share our life today

October 12, 1995

*

Careers

My first career rests in my heart
I watched my children grow
My babies brought me so much joy
More than they could know

And then, a lilting melody
Echoed in my ear
Teaching 'do, re, mi'
Became my next career

Music filled the air
Oh hear it resonate
While savoring sweet sounds
A journey lay in wait

A path would take me back to school
Through sun and clouds and rain
In search of endless knowledge
I found I had a brain

This led me to the business world
A job from nine to five
I left my cozy little nest
And off to work I'd drive

Once again the road ahead
May lead to something new
When I grow up, what shall I be?
I still don't have a clue

*

Somerset Valley Orchestra

Every Thursday evening we meet at Bound Brook High
A group of music lovers—oh my, oh my, we try

Don is our director—he really knows his stuff
At times he's very gentle and other times he's tough

I can't say that I blame him—it must be hard to hear
A squeak, a toot that's out of place, a jolt upon the ear

The brass is overwhelming—oh hear the trumpets blare
Their overtones are ringing—the clarinets despair

Now Don defines the music explaining in detail
Creative, subtle nuances—let artistry prevail

And music is a language, a simple lexicon
Translated into English—just keep your eye on Don

At times we're not quite with it—we try for our best tone
The 'pro' sits back and rolls his eyes and then lets out a groan

But when we have our concert, we say a little prayer
We rise to the occasion and music fills the air

This brings us joy and happiness when all is said and done
And here's a little bonus—it's such a lot of fun

And to our faithful patrons, a message we impart
May you go forth with lilting joy and music in your heart

*

The Journey

I gaze out of my window
Behold a graceful deer
This has been my domicile
My home for many a year

The walls embrace my soul
With sweet serenity
I'm captured by the charm
Of warm complacency

But life beats on in cadence
Adventures are to take
Life has new beginnings
New memories to make

All too soon it's time for change
The earth does not stand still
The best rewards may yet to be
Just beyond the hill

*

Moving Day

A journey lies ahead
To places far away
A tender feeling in my heart
Goodbye to yesterday

Boxes line the room
Neatly in a row
A treasure of sweet memories
And furniture to go

Tis written in the stars
Beyond the Zodiac
This is moving day
There is no turning back

From lofty, noble mountains
To awesome, boundless ocean
Adventure lies ahead
And bittersweet emotion

Goodbye my lovely mountains
My journey takes me far
And to my dearest friends
A poignant au revoir

*

The House

Once upon a time
In a village far away
We dwelt within a house
For many and many a day

Memories were made
We watched our children grow
Joy would grace my soul
And pain of loss I'd know

Then with little warning
Time had swiftly flown
I found an empty house
And I was all alone

The unknown lay before me
My head would lead the way
My heart would shed a tear
Goodbye to yesterday

A new tomorrow greets me
As I journey far and wide
I think about the little house
That holds my heart inside

Tis nestled in the woods
And echoes tears and laughter
The house holds golden moments
And memories ever after

*

My Birthday Gift

A glowing golden image
Etched in memory
Warms my heart evermore
A vision I still see

It was a special birthday
With grandkids I adore
We shared a day at the lake
To cherish evermore

Jody was a girl of nine
Mitchell barely one
She tended to him lovingly
Beneath a golden sun

I watched them romp along the shore
The sky was getting low
Shadows on the waters
Cast an awesome glow

Bending over Mitchell
A scene I'll not forget
Stood my darling Jody Ann
In a love filled silhouette

Behold this priceless image
To me a work of art
My birthday gift—I thought
Tis nestled in my heart

Love, Grandma Chrissy

*

35

Passages

Kitty Cat

Once we had a kitty cat, cute as she could be
She'd curl around your ankle; she'd climb up on your knee

A member of the family—sweet cuddly calico
A furry, purring butterball prancing to and fro

One day we couldn't find her—"O where could kitty be?"
Until we heard woeful meows from high up in a tree

We called; we coaxed; we pleaded; she would not leave her perch
Day One passed with no results; for rescue, we would search

We called the A-S-P-C-A; "What are we to do?"
Try this and that and everything, but still no luck—Day Two

Volunteers and firemen came with trucks and stuff
But in great dismay they found no ladder high enough

We hoped to find a woodsman, one who'd climb the tree
Woeful meowing broke our hearts and lasted through Day Three

Day Four brought a thunderstorm; a fierce bolt shook the skies
And soon a scrawny dragged out cat stood before our eyes

*

Stray

One fine day a dog appeared / On my neighbors' lawn
It remained throughout the night / And yet was there at dawn

The husband said, "Remember / We really have enough
Furry little creatures" / He warned his wife, "be tough."

For days on end the stray remained / An ever-present sight
Until one day it wasn't there / Something wasn't right

Someone had reported / To the A-S-P-CA
We then came to realize / They took the dog away

The wife, my friend Virginia / Now became upset
And headed for the pound / The dog she went to get

This noble beast was saved from doom / And was not put to sleep
The husband now relented / And it was theirs to keep

But then my friend embraced a thought / That echoed in her mind
This once abandoned animal / Perhaps, could lead the blind

And so as fate would have it / The Seeing Eye ordained
This loyal, gentle creature / Was welcomed to be trained

The pup, so eager to obey / Displayed her pedigree
Born to serve a master / This was her destiny

Now here's a little footnote / That I would like to post
The husband—he lamented / He missed the dog the most

*

Virginia
(Ode to a Friend)

The first time I saw her she held a babe in arm
She introduced herself to me warmly and with charm

Little did we realize what great friends we'd become
The path between our houses—well traveled to and from

We'd have our morning chitchat when the school bus drove away
I don't know where it came from—there was so much to say

She had a love of living things, beautiful to see
A stray, a broken wing, she nurtured tenderly

Her wry sense of humor echoed here and there
And she had a way with words—concepts we would share

We faced our daily happenings—good and bad would flow
With love and pride of offspring we watched our children grow

Then from out of nowhere fate called out her name
She waged her war with dignity in a poignant futile game

Now the path is overgrown—the path of long ago
I think about my bosom friend and our first 'hello'

*

Pope John Paul II

Summer had been hot and dry—our reservoirs were low
We prayed for rain to ease the drought and make the flowers grow

But now the Pope was coming—we hoped the rain would wait
Our choir planned to sing for him on this historic date

Our bus left home in pouring rain with nothing we could do
Wishful thinking of the day—that gray skies would turn blue

Yellow buses everywhere—they came to see the Pope
The Meadowlands were teeming with those of faith and hope

The crowds were quite spectacular—excitement filled the air
And then the Pope arrived at last with fanfare and with flare

Voices rang Hosanna as a cloud burst shook the sky
As though in answer to our song, a message from on high

Multi-cultures billowed in sweeping rapturous sound
The roar of joyous people rippled round and round

And then the children took the stage—so beautiful to see
With sounds that echoed innocence in a lilting melody

Drenched in rain from head to toe—our music sopping wet
We struggled so to turn each page while joy embraced us yet

John Paul's voice now echoed across the Meadowlands
He spoke of rain, a sign of life, the poor and helping hands

Soon the Mass was ended—time to go in peace
With hope within our hearts where blessings never cease

I remember during Mass, I looked high above
And there across the rain drenched sky—a soaring peaceful dove

October 5, 1995
*

42

Princess

Once there was a princess, regal and serene
A shy and pretty maiden, the essence of a queen
Her prince had come one fateful day—true love would prevail
Their wedding was magnificent, a real life fairy tale

Soon the words would resonate—glad tidings far and wide
News rang out, a darling heir was at his mother's side
The new prince brought such happiness and overwhelming joy
And then the joy was doubled with another darling boy

Paparazzi chased her—they gave her little space
They stifled her existence with cameras in her face
She grew in classic beauty with a loving smile
She grew in poise and dignity—a paragon of style

And then a hint of sadness filtered through her eyes
The fairy tale was crumbling to everyone's surprise
Her private pain and agony were splattered everywhere
Lack of private moments led her to despair

In time a ray of sunshine brought happiness at last
A glow of love encircled her—it seemed her pain had past
Of course the world was watching and wishing she would find
The one true love she longed for and some peace of mind

But as fate would have it, it was not to be
Her life was snatched away from her—a poignant tragedy
Many millions loved her; many hearts unfurled
Lady Diana Spencer—Princess of the world

*

Billy

Twas the night before Christmas
And all was quite right
When he entered the world
To his parents' delight

He grew and he grew
To a fine looking lad
In so many ways
A lot like his dad

A man of rich taste
And elegant things
With a magical spark
That Manhattan brings

A model of style
And meticulous dress
His manner and presence
Are sure to impress

A soul of sweet mystery
Behind a calm screen
The path to communicate
A message machine

Now here is a wish
For all the years through
May peace fill his heart
And sweet dreams come true

*

Tragedy

The letter came on Friday
With eagerness we read
Our rapt anticipation
So quickly turned to dread

Oh what were we reading
This surely can't be real
His pain engulfed the pages
Pain we now would feel

We tried so hard to find him
And then the policeman came
We searched his eyes and wondered
What words he would proclaim

He spoke the words so softly
He told us of his fate
This boy with so much promise
Embraced the Golden Gate

Our hearts would never be the same
How could we miss the signs
His cheerful words had hidden
Pain between the lines

*

Lost Son

Many, many years had past since last they said Goodbye
Sands of time would steal away and years would quickly fly

A father and his little son were destined to part
The father went his separate way, a twinge within his heart

Time marched on in cadence with every passing day
The boy grew into manhood, the father's hair turned gray

The man so longed to see his son—perhaps a warm embrace
He dreamed about a joyous day when they'd meet face to face

And then one day it came to pass—fate opened up a door
Beyond those years of wondering their lives would touch once more

As the door was opened, excitement filled the air
And there before the father's eyes—an answer to a prayer

The room became engulfed with his pride and joy
Framed by the doorway stood his long lost boy

The moment was electric—he knew not what to do
The father now embraced his son—his sweetest dream came true

*

Good Neighbor

In winter I am stranded
When heavy snows take hold
The driveway is impassable
The scene is stark and cold

The beauty of the trees
Draped in crystal dress
Belies its cunning nature
Spawning stressfulness

Then one day I see him
Plowing through the snow
It is an act of kindness
From a man I hardly know

Up and down the driveway
He clears the snow away
I really don't expect it
I don't know what to say

It is reassuring
To have a neighbor near
One that I can count on
He makes that very clear

In deep appreciation
My heart is warmed indeed
In turn I hope that I could help
Someone else in need

*

Adventures in Condoland

I ventured into Condoland
Not knowing what I'd find
I found a group of friendly folk
Gentle, sweet and kind

The setting is serene
In a rustic countryside
A lovely corner of the world
A touch of nature's pride

There's a pool and a clubhouse
A fitness center too
Options here and there
With many things to do

And let us not forget
The chores of long ago
No more mowing lawns
No more shoveling snow

It's feeling more like home
This is the place for me
I love my new adventure
And my condo family

*

Brookfield

Brookfield Glen and Brookfield Homes
Share a lovely place
Warm and picture perfect
We dwell in its embrace

Behold this 'Rockwell' neighborhood
Folks amble on their way
With waves and smiles and greetings
On a warm and golden day

There is a man from Brookfield Homes
A pleasant guy named Ken
Who waves 'hello' to all of us
The folks from Brookfield Glen

One day to his surprise
In answer to 'hello'
A lady stopped to greet him
A Glen gal named Flo

It warms my heart to see this
Neighbors tried and true
Who share this corner of the earth
And the red, white and blue

I'm thankful for this place called home
Underneath the sun
And for the folks I get to know
Neighbors—one on one

*

The Glen Gazette

Hear Ye! Hear Ye! One and All
Glad tidings resonate
We introduce *The Glen Gazette*
A voice to celebrate

We'll speak of timely topics
Of items here and there
And tell about activities
And give you news to share

Contributions welcomed
Questions, ideas, art
A little bit of laughter
A message from your heart

Hear Ye! Hear Ye! One and All
When all is said and done
The Glen Gazette will echo
With news for everyone

*

Gigs Are Us

Here a gig, there a gig / This is what we do
A group of music lovers / Will play a song for you

Listen to the sounds / Here and there a toot
Listen to the melody / O hear the magic flute

Clarinets resonate / And tones caress the ear
Let gladness fill your heart / And worries disappear

Trumpet bells are raised / A fanfare greets the soul
O Hear the oom-pah-pah / O Hear the drumbeat roll

Feel the steady cadence / The rhythm of the beat
Makes you want to dance / Makes you tap your feet

Magic fills the air / When our work is done
We play with heart and soul / And it's so much fun

To our loyal patrons / A wish we now impart
May you go forth with lilting song / And music in your heart

Revel in the joys of life / Music is a plus
Our concert band is here for you / Remember 'Gigs Are Us'

*

Music

Music is a language
Of prayer and romance
Music is the heartbeat
Of song and dance

Music is a common thread
A universal link
That reaches round the world
From one cup we drink

O hear a grand concerto
Or a simple melody
Blended tones resonate
In sweet harmony

We celebrate with music
O hear a joyous choir
We celebrate the gift of life
With spirit, soul and fire

Music is to sound
What color is to sight
It takes the soul from darkness
And brings it into light

And to those we cherish
O let the music start
A melody of love
To share what's in our heart

*

Twelve Tones

Twelve tones resonate
They form a melody
A simple tune, a lively dance
The grandest symphony

From the Middle Ages
They echo through the years
Gregorian Chant to Mozart
And roving balladeers

The genius of a Gershwin
'Rhapsody in Blue'
And Beatles' Rock and Roll
Oh hear, 'Love Me Do'

Twelve tones speak volumes
Of history and art
Of cultures round the world
And feelings of the heart

Tones arranged by masters
In a lyric paradigm
From folk songs to the classics
Stand the test of time

*

Chasing Rainbows

Chasing rainbows round the world
Where work is more like play
A dream job for my darling child
Adventure far away

As a mom I wonder
Will my dear one thrive?
All I ever want for you
A job from nine to five

Free Spirit is your mantra
Far beyond the seas
In a journey chasing rainbows
And building memories

No one does it better
This, I must admit
Tracking down those rainbows
For you—a perfect fit

My darling precious child
My love I give to you
I celebrate your lilting heart
May all your dreams come true

A poignant message resonates
With every passing day
We teach our children how to walk
And then—to fly away

Mom
*

People

People

We walk through life mid people
Cross paths along the way
Some will touch our lives
Forever and a day

Others—brief encounters
We may soon forget
They may seem insignificant
Of little note, and yet

With each step along the way
Something's left behind
A tender act of kindness
A thought that grips the mind

With every stage in life
Families are made
Fellow workers, concert bands
Teams, as games are played

All too soon it's time for change
We may drift apart
But special folks are nestled
In the corner of our heart

*

Mister Friendly
(A Guy Named Joe)

I call him Mister Friendly
A gentleman is he
He spreads a bit of sunshine
In our community

When I see him on the road
To myself I say
'Here comes Mister Friendly
He'll brighten up my day'

A simple, kind 'hello'
Is music to my ear
Like a lilting melody
Echoing sweet cheer

It is so refreshing
In this world of woe
To meet a pleasant fellow
A friendly guy named Joe

*

Choir Master

Now here's a man of elegance
On the podium he stands
He is our choirmaster
He waves his arms and hands

He reaches deep within our souls
And brings forth rhapsody
Music of the masters
Rings out in harmony

Tenors and basses
Deeply resonate
Sopranos sing like angels
Altos modulate

"Now watch for your crescendos
And accents," he will say
He rolls his eyes so patiently
And then he starts to pray

He rounds his lips and puckers
A fish he imitates
He pulls upon his hair and beard
The choir resonates

From deep within our souls
He makes the music flow
A tribute to our maestro
Choirmaster Joe

*

Dear Friends
(Roberta & Dave)

Many years have passed
Since our last goodbye
There was no way of knowing
How quickly years would fly

We shared a bit of yesterday
O so long ago
We built a cache of memories
We watched our children grow

Then with little fanfare
We drifted far apart
With echoes of sweet tenderness
Deep within the heart

Sands of time have slipped away
And now it's plain to see
Friendship is a treasure
A sweet amenity

O sing a song of friendship
And let it resonate
Our lives have touched once more
O let us celebrate

*

KFC

Brookfield Glen and Brookfield Homes
Share a bit of space
A lovely corner of the world
Indeed—a lovely place

I meet some pleasant folks
When I take my daily walk
At times we take a moment
And have a little talk

But how will I remember
Everybody's name
I have to be creative
I play a silly game

Kentucky is for Kathy
It comes from KFC
Fried is for Frank
And Chicken is for me

It helps me to remember
In travels far and wide
A name I'll not forget
Poor Frank—he is Fried

In my journey through the seasons
With each step along the way
Folks like Frank and Kathy
Brighten up my day

*

Barbara

Memories take me back
To a classroom long ago
'Friendship' seeds were sown
And time would see them grow

Barbara is her name
I call her Bobbi-boo
She's bright and sweet and kind
And easy-going too

This is a special lady
A stand-up kind of gal
A lady with a heart
I'm proud to call my pal

We would keep in touch
With a luncheon here and there
Echoes of sweet chatter
Always filled the air

While sands of time slipped away
A lovely 'flower' grew
A lifetime friendship blossomed
Beneath a sky of blue

I think about that day
In that classroom long ago
A cherished friend touched my life
With her first 'hello'

*

The Brookfield Walkers

They spread a bit of sunshine
With a bright 'hello'
Along the road in Brookfield
That's Herb and Dick and Joe

I see them through the seasons
When snows caress the panes
And when the days grow longer
In springtime when it rains

I see them in the summer
Beneath the blazing sun
They take their morning stroll
A new day has begun

And in the crisp, cool air
When days are drenched in gold
They trod between the houses
Where autumn scenes unfold

When all is said and done
There's one more thing to say
Something I have noticed
Gentlemen, are they

*

Old Friends

Thirty years—can it be?
Since last we said goodbye
There was no way of knowing
How quickly years would fly

Two young couples sharing space
So very long ago
We laughed, we cried together
In friendship we would grow

But then as often happens
We drifted far apart
We had not even noticed
A feeling in the heart

It lay deeply in our souls
And never did we see
Till now we've come to realize
We were a family

As they drove up I strained to look
With care I must admit
And then to my delight I found
They had not changed a bit

And now our lives have touched once more
Full circle made today
We'll keep in touch from this day on
When friends are far away

*

Aunt Marge

Passages of milestones
In the journey through a year
Stir up poignant moments
And perhaps a little tear

Remembering a lady
Of poise and dignity
Epitome of graciousness
And family loyalty

She never missed a birthday
A wedding or a birth
She always sent warm wishes
With love for all it's worth

Indeed a family treasure
A jewel from the start
She holds a very special place
In the corner of my heart

*

Beulah

Now Beulah is a lady
I very much respect
Warm and sweet and genuine
As you might expect

Born in Pennsylvania
Raised on a farm
A bona fide country gal
With old fashioned charm

She spent a lot of years
At New York City's door
Shades of city culture
Touch her ever more

There was a certain someone
A partner if you please
A gentle man named Barney
They shared some memories

Her brothers and her sisters
Their sons and daughters too
Bespeak her love of family
To her heart she's true

There's another certain someone
A frisky dividend
Devoted and affectionate
Rags her little friend

Now we are here to wish her well
A milestone marks this year
Happy Birthday Beulah
Hear it loud and clear

*

Diane

Quiet footsteps in the hall
A smile, a bright 'hello'
Behold our own sweet Diane
Today she's on the go

She's off to see that little guy
That she's so nuts about
He's smart, he's cute, he's funny
He's perfect, there's no doubt

But then again, that's Diane
Her family brings her joy
There's Alex and there's Cate
And Max, the little boy

Lisa is her darling child
The apple of her eye
And Michail, Lisa's love
Is one more family tie

In the album of her life
Mid snapshots here and there
See her sister Carol
Sweet memories, they share

There's Mike who shares her world
A standup kind of guy
He putters here and there
There's nothing he won't try

But now we're here to celebrate
And sing the best we can
From those of us who love you
'Happy Birthday! Sweet Diane'

*

Ode to the Sullivans

Kudos to the Sullivans
So long overdue
To Joan and to Denis
Gems in our milieu

What they do looks easy
But let's make no mistake
Themes and deadlines loom
It's not a piece of cake

A giant jigsaw puzzle
Scattered everywhere
Somehow comes together
For all of us to share

Mark and Sasha breathe a sigh
While lending full support
Members of the household
You know—the purry sort

And in the family album
Snapshots tell a story
See Lisa and see Karen
The Sullivans' pride and glory

Kudos to the Sullivans
We shall not forget
The flower of a job well done
Our own Glen Gazette

*

A Couple Named Alu

Listen up '40 Folks'
I give you now the news
A tale of hospitality
A tale of the Alus

There's Mike and there's Dorian
Nice as they can be
Cheery Mike and Dorian
With a kitty on her knee

They open up their home
With grace and style
And bring us all together
With a contagious smile

A sense of humor serves them well
Chuckles here and there
A clever word with tongue-in-cheek
A little joke to share

Thanks to Mike and Dorian
They've opened up their door
And welcomed us as family
We couldn't ask for more

Listen up everyone
A message now for you
Building 40 celebrates
A couple named Alu

*

Ren
(Master of the Wheel)

Village folks board the bus
With smiles from ear to ear
They know that Ren is at the wheel
There's not a thing to fear

He is a skillful driver
Of that there is no doubt
Weaving through the traffic
Round and round about

Master of the wheel is he
Cruising here and there
Squeezing through the tightest spots
Without an inch to spare

He knows where all the potholes are
And the bumps as well
He spares us from a jolt or two
More than words can tell

O hear that beep, beep, beep
As he backs up to your door
And then he lends a helping hand
With packages galore

Echoes ring out loud and clear
O hear the people say
"Thank you Ren! You are the best!"
As he drives away

*

Copilot

There is a certain fellow
Who rides upon our bus
A bona fide copilot
Yet, he's one of us

He is the driver's helper
As he calls out, 'all is clear'
Along with other tidbits
That echo from the rear

'Cut the heat,' resonates
When it gets too hot
And when it comes to laughter
He's Johnny on the spot

He takes note of who's on board
A number kept in mind
Then when we are homeward bound
No one's left behind

A kindly sort of fellow
Master of the game
A bona fide copilot
And Kevin is his name

*

Pat

Together we have traveled far
There's so much world to see
She moves so fast—I look around
And say, 'Hey, wait for me'

If you go riding in her car
You're in for quite a treat
But let me first remind you
To hold on to your seat

And then when lunch time rolls around
We all look at her plate
The salads she brings in each day
Just make us salivate

Water, water everywhere
Patricia's favorite drink
A beverage quite compatible
To keep one in the pink

Tall and classy is this gal
As friends go she's the top
She is a special lady
The daughter of Clancy the cop

*

Richie's Song

He stands upon the podium
See that hammer swing
Richie takes the stage
And a lilting song takes wing

When jobs pile up around me
I'm glad that he is near
The pinging of his hammer
Is music to my ear

He does so many things
That's Richie on the spot
He fixes this and that
And gives it all he's got

A decent sort of fellow
Craftsman of the day
'Job well done' echoes
Throughout his resume

When you hear that truck
Chug, chug, chug along
Know he's come to save the day
O hear it—'Richie's Song'

*

George

Hear this heartfelt tribute
Let it resonate
A tribute to a gentle man
Whose life we celebrate

A wave, a smile, a greeting
A chuckle here and there
A tasty bowl of soup
He made for us to share

See him in his baseball cap
A deck of cards in hand
This pleasant sort of fellow
None finer in the land

He served his family well
And to his heart was true
Love for Carol, Bruce and Bob
And the firstborn, Sue

Now he rests with Scotty
Who left so long ago
Little angel in his heart
Where love would grow and grow

Through the many years
In the portrait of his life
Behold his lifelong sweetheart
Pat, his loving wife

*

Sue

O hear that chitter, chatter
A lilting, rhythmic sound
It echoes like a melody
When Susan is around

She is one cool cookie
With a voice that's most sincere
She speaks her mind with candor
To those who lend an ear

She's also very funny
And witty as can be
She brings about a chuckle
Or maybe two or three

Now here's a tiny tidbit
Little known but true
Behind that cool cucumber
Behold a warm, Sweet Sue

*

Love

Valentine
(A Little Love Story)

"Will you be my Valentine?"
It's just a little phrase
Some folks may remember
All their livelong days

Behold a fine young lad
Who echoes every word
And the little lass who hears him
Loving what she's heard

Time goes by until one day
She's walking down the aisle
Remembering those words
Her sweetheart wears a smile

Will the beauty of the phrase
See them through each year?
Will it enhance the happy times?
Will it wipe away a tear?

And when they reach their golden days
Will words be said anew?
"Will you be my Valentine?
Forever—I love you"

*

Snapshots

Behold a brilliant sunset
A mountain capped in snow
But something else warms my heart
And sets me all aglow

Love between two people
Is a precious thing to me
A cradled babe in mother's arms
A sight I love to see

Picture this—young sisters
Giggling in fun
And it's so nice to see
A man embrace his son

I love to see a young lad
Stick up for his little brother
And see two loyal friends
Stand by one another

Friends, lovers, soul mates
An image to behold
The image tells a story
The sweetest story told

In the album of my world
In travels far and wide
A picture tells what matters most
A loved one by your side

*

Sacred Ties

A mother and her daughter
A father and his son
Those we love are everything
When all is said and done

They bring the sweetest joy
They bring the deepest pain
Like sunshine on a golden day
And all too soon the rain

The lifelong bond of sisters
And brothers through the years
A friend's undying loyalty
In laughter and through tears

Vows between two people
As they venture forth in life
That stand the test of time
In good times and in strife

Rippling in the wind
There's a ribbon in the sky
That weaves a tale of love
With every sacred tie

*

Sweet Blessings

When Jody was a baby
I'd look at her and smile
Thank heaven for sweet blessings
That make it all worthwhile

She is my baby's baby
Little doll in pink
Thank heaven for little girls
We share a special wink

Meanwhile across the land
Another family
Was counting its blessings
With baby number three

They called the cherub Kevin
This little Gemini
He grew to be a fine young man
A stand-up kind of guy

In a journey through the seasons
Little did they know
Their paths would meet one day
And seeds of love would grow

Cherish now the moment
As they start their life anew
With promise of sweet blessings
And lofty dreams come true

April 18, 2007
Love, Grandma Chrissy

*

A Little Fairy Tale

Once upon a time
Along the Delaware
A school bus trod the roads
And clamor filled the air

Amid the noisy cherubs
Sat a lad and lass
Images of school days
In cadence time would pass

Fast forward to another scene
A vision of today
See Erica and Sean
Her prince had come her way

Little did they realize
Their hearts would beat as one
'New fragrance to the flowers
New gladness to the sun'

May beauty fill their earth
And love grow sweet with time
May life become a warm embrace
In a golden paradigm

Those of us who love them
Wish them smiles and laughter
In a kingdom where they'll live
Happily ever after

November 11, 2005
Love, Grandma Chrissy

*

Glad Toddings

Hear Ye! Hear Ye! One and all
Glad tidings fill the air
Michelle and Todd now speak the words
Their vows—a solemn prayer

Together they make music
Here and there a toot
Listen to the melody
O hear the magic flute

May precious moments fill their hearts
As love grows sweet with time
May life become a warm embrace
In a golden paradigm

Those of us who love them
Join in celebration
With wishes for sweet blessings
In joyous jubilation

Hear Ye! Hear Ye! One and all
The news across the land
As man and wife they greet the world
Together hand in hand

October 29, 2011
Love, G'ma Chrissy

*

Hand in Hand

A couple holding hands
An image tinged in love
Radiating tenderness
A blessing from above

Walking hand in hand
With every step they take
Partners on a journey
Gestures that they make

A silent message rings
In sweet harmony
Words within the heart
A soulful melody

The couple may not realize
While every day they share
The hand they hold is priceless
An answer to a prayer

*

Symphony of Love

All the world is longing
For a precious kind of love
The kind that weaves sweet memories
A blessing from above

All the world is searching
For places in the sun
Looking for a haven
Where two will equal one

Beyond a lofty rainbow
One reaches for a goal
To find that special someone
That warm and kindred soul

In the magic of the moment
When true love is found
A symphony of love
Echoes round and round

*

Wedding Song

When chosen paths cross
Birds begin to sing
Names become entwined
Amid a golden ring

Hearts embrace each other
Forever come what may
They step forward hand in hand
To share a life today

Love between two people
Is the greatest gift in life
A blessed treasure in the heart
The love of man and wife

May magic moments fill their days
As life unfolds anew
With love that stands the test of time
And happy dreams come true

*

Pollyanna Speaks

Our lives have touched forever more
Pollyanna speaks
There is a love within the heart
That everybody seeks

Understanding virtue, vice
Kindred souls are we
A special kind of friendship
That keeps the spirit free

Blending love and friendship
Deep within the heart
It doesn't happen every day
A blessing to impart

Sharing, caring, tenderness
Sparks that will not die
Blossoms of companionship
That grow as time goes by

*

Jack and Sara

Memories of childhood
Long ago and far away
Awaken poignant moments
Etched in yesterday

Though Jack endured adversity
While boyhood passed him by
He grew to be a fine young man
A stand-up kind of guy

Meanwhile, growing up
In a Pennsylvania town
Behold a sweet young Sara
With siblings all around

One day their paths would meet
And it was plain to see
Jack and Sara hand in hand
Their love was meant to be

Many years have past
Since they said, "I do"
"I love her more today," says Jack
"Indeed I like her too"

In the scheme of things
When all is said and done
Behold lifelong sweethearts
Beneath a golden sun

*

The Vows

Two score and ten
A milestone to be sure
A milestone in a journey
Of love that would endure

Behold the bride and groom
In a scene from yesterday
Standing at the altar
With solemn words to say

The words would ever resonate
As time consumed the years
Amid a loving family
With smiles and sometimes tears

And now behold another scene
Before the world they stand
Renewing sacred wedding vows
Together hand in hand

*

To Love Another Day

When love is shared it tends to grow
Into a special bond
It touches every part of you
Like ripples in a pond

But love not shared tends to fade
Until it comes to die
Then there's nothing left to do
Except to say goodbye

Days go by and soon you find
Those with love to give
Are filled with hope and confidence
For love is why we live

Life goes on and those who have
Love to give away
Are by far the lucky ones
They'll love another day

*

A Father's Love

It warms my heart to see
A man embrace his son
From babyhood to manhood
In trials and times of fun

And through the years an image
Of camaraderie
Fishing trips and ball games
A montage of glee

Now picture this—a dance
With daddy's little girl
Her tiny feet rest on his
Around the room they swirl

Fast forward to another scene
A scene that steals the day
A tear trips down his cheek
As he gives the bride away

In the drama of life
A father's role is clear
It takes center stage
With every passing year

*

The Wind Between My Toes
(A Love Story)

I love your gentle, warm embrace
I love a long stemmed rose
But what I love most of all
The wind between my toes

Roses are red—flower of love
Violets are bathed in blue
But look at my pink tootsies
The breeze is streaming through

These tootsies are so happy
Love is everywhere
Big toe, little toe, and those between
Ten toes in the air

And so my love I tell you
While in our hearts love grows
The sweetest joy in my life
The wind between my toes

*

Smiles

The Art of Cooking

The art of cooking is a gift
Now I'm not one to boast
But no one does it better
I make the finest toast

See me in my kitchen
See me slave and toil
Of this, I'm very confident
Water, I can boil

Often when I'm hungry
Mid growls from my belly
There's that good old standby
Peanut butter and jelly

In searching through my recipes
I'm sure to find a winner
"Oh, what the heck," I tell myself
"I'll have a TV Dinner"

Here's something to remember
From culinary school
A gadget that can open cans
Is a handy tool

In the scheme of things
I have a sneaky hunch
That when this gift was handed out
I was out to lunch

*

Busy Doing Nothing

I get up in the morning—so much lies ahead
I have a list of things to do before I go to bed
I take a morning stroll and meet a staunch brigade
The dog walkers march with pooches on parade

After breakfast, email calls and Spam is everywhere
Oh and by the way—a game of solitaire
Phone calls are in order—press this, press that, I'm told
And what can I accomplish while languishing on hold

Is morning gone already? Time to grab a bite
There is so much I have to do before it turns to night
Shall I go to market? Are we low on bread?
Or shall I read the paper and relax instead?

While I scan the paper, puzzles catch my eye
Crosswords and Sudoku—I'll give them all a try
Talk shows fill my day and sometimes things I've heard
Make me shout in protest but no one hears a word

Must not forget my music—here and there a toot
I know I'll drive my neighbors nuts if I don't use the mute
Now it's time for Oprah—I wonder who's her guest
I'll watch the parts of interest—I have to keep abreast

Here we are it's dinnertime—I'll set aside my book
And grab a little sandwich—there is no time to cook
When all is said and done time will slip away
And so to bed till morning and another busy day

*

Krazy Quilts and Green Bananas

I step into a room
With pace and much ado
But then I stand and wonder why
And I don't have a clue

Broken mirrors everywhere
Here and there a crack
That can't be my reflection
Oh my aching back

I met a friend the other day
We spoke of days gone by
And things we used to do
When we could touch the sky

"I'd like to start a quilt," she said
"But there's no guarantee
That I will ever finish it
Alas! Woe is me!"

The years have slipped away
We've traveled far and wide
The road ahead may challenge us
With a bit of a bumpy ride

"But everything will turn out well"
O hear sweet Pollyanna
"Go ahead—make that quilt!
Go buy that green banana!"

*

Tasty Tarts

Now here's a tasty recipe
A favorite of mine
A secret in our family
And sweet as any wine

Take a cup of sugar
Or is it two or three?
Add one drop of water
And stir thoroughly

Add a dozen eggs
And a pinch of flour
Mix it all together
And bake for an hour

When all is said and done
This tart will make you drool
And here's another secret
Oh hear it! April Fool!

*

Grandmas Never Say No

I love to be with grandma
It's such a lot of fun
I get to do so many things
I skip, I jump, I run

When we go out shopping
I get a red balloon
And when we bake a cake
I get to lick the spoon

Grandma lets me pet the cat
And listen to it purr
She lets me hug the dog
It's all okay with her

I love to go to grandma's house
I can't wait to go
I do the things I want to do
Grandmas don't say 'no'

John
(Age 4)

*

Daddy's Little Packer

When I was just a little girl
I idolized my Dad
And cherished time I shared with him
The best I ever had

I would sit beside him
As he watched his favorite game
He rooted for his team
And I would do the same

"Pick a team," he said one day
"That you can call your own
A team that you can root for
One that's yours alone"

He rattled off a list of names
From the NFL
I couldn't choose the Giants
I knew that all too well

I listened very carefully
While munching on my crackers
And then an echo loud and clear
"That's it—the Green Bay Packers!"

I became a lifelong fan
And loved it from the start
But most of all my time with Dad
Tis nestled in my heart

*

Joey and the Bandit

They trod the roads at daybreak
When the sun begins to shine
Greeting folks along the way
They walk a crafty line

They stroll along at midday
And steal a breath of air
That's Joey and the Bandit
They strut without a care

And then again at dusk
When the moon is peeking through
They pocket golden moments
And snatch a smile or two

Partners in 'crime'
Together come what may
The Bandit wags a happy tail
And steals your heart away

*

Broken Cookies

When we were very little
Times were oh so tough
We longed for any goodies
But never had enough

There was a cookie factory
In our neighborhood
A sweet aroma filled the air
It always smelled so good

The workers tended to their jobs
Busily all day
Boxing all the cookies
And tossing dregs away

A certain lady on the job
Came to realize
How we longed for goodies
She saw it in our eyes

And then a day I'll not forget
A knock upon our door
There stood the lady
With cookies galore

Though they were broken cookies
We savored every crumb
I still love broken cookies
Yummy! Yummy! Yum!

*

Buy One—Get One

I can't resist a sale
Even though I try
When I see a bargain
I get that urge to buy

See my store of peanut butter
Lots more than I need
The price was right and now
An army I can feed

Magic bullets stock my shelves
Tiny dynamos
Busters of cholesterol
Incredible Cheerios

'Buy one—get one free'
Catchy and concise
But all I want is one
One at half the price

Some TV ads are clever
Others get my goat
Thank heaven for this gadget
My little old remote

*

Press One Now

Press one, press two, or maybe three / Round and round we go
In search of some assistance / I need to reach a 'pro'

I listen to all options / Now I sing the blues
Eeny, meeny, miny, mo / Which one shall I choose?

At last, a human voice / Oh no—a foreign tongue
How will I understand? / By now, the phone, I've flung

Patience now, I tell myself / Oh let me not be rude
I want to fix my problem / To the phone I'm glued

Step by step we move along / Clicking here and there
Echoes of sweet promises / Begin to fill the air

I follow all instructions / Download this and that
While we wait and wait / We begin to chat

Now I feel a little guilt / I acted like a snob
After all, I tell myself / She's there to do a job

I learn some things about her / And she, about me
And yes she fixed my problem / I'm pleased as I can be

*

Atlantic City

They board the cheery bus
And share a bit of news
Years have slipped away
They've paid their lifelong dues

Now's the time to have some fun
Bingo is not enough
Time to let their hair down
Time to strut their stuff

Walkers, canes, creaky bones
Atlantic City scene
Seniors all determined
To reach that slot machine

The one armed bandits resonate
Cranking here and there
A chance to break the bank
And be a millionaire

When all is said and done
Dreams shall never die
O see that lively spirit
Reaching for the sky

*

I'd Rather Have a Bench

'How shall we spend this money?'
Asks Joan with a smile
'Let's make our neighbors happy
Let's make it all worthwhile'

'We could buy some paintings
And decorate each palace'
'I'd rather have a bench'
Pipes up our own sweet Alice

'We could purchase a projector
And get to watch a show
Make use of our own clubhouse
And not have far to go'

When all is said and done
And we all agree
'I'd rather have a bench'
From the peanut gallery

*

Billy This and Billy That

It's Billy this and Billy that
And Billy fix the lock
It's Billy this and Billy that
And Billy fix the clock

He does so many things for me
At times I have to wait
But when all is said and done
I do appreciate

It's Billy this and Billy that
Let's take a trip to Spain
It's Billy this and Billy that
Let's see that rainy plain

To me he is Sir William
High upon a hill
With vice and virtue rolled in one
To me he is my Bill

*

Bocce

It's that time of year
All across the Glen
Bocce fever's in the air
Spreading once again

Get that arm in shape
Brush up on your aim
Close in on that polino
The object of the game

O Hear the cheering fans
In the peanut gallery
Rooting for their team
In camaraderie

Ken is up on deck
Look at that technique
Style and grace and skill
He's on a winning streak

Here's something to remember
When all is said and done
When good folks get together
It's such a lot of fun

*

Brookfield Rules

Before you buy a condo
Here at Brookfield Glen
There is a special rule
Made up way back when

You cannot be a grouch
No Scrooges are allowed
We look for sunny days
Without a single cloud

And here's another rule
In Brookfield Glen enclave
When meeting passersby
We're all obliged to wave

Never burn your toast
It could start a riot
A piercing, screeching siren
Will shatter peace and quiet

When going for a stroll
Give a nice 'hello'
To those you meet along the way
Some you'll get to know

And one more rule to mention
In Pollyanna Land
Remember, we are family
Together hand in hand

*

The Line Dancers

We're not the famed Rockettes
We're not like Fred Astaire
But we give it all we have
With gusto and with flair

Vines—scissors—pivots
The lexicon of dance
Echoes round the room
While we Glen Gals prance

Cha-cha-cha—one, two, three
Back and forth we sway
Oops—I think I messed it up
I'm facing the wrong way

'Practice makes perfect'
O hear it resonate
The spirit of Terpsichore
Shall rise and emanate

Right step, left toe
Across the floor we glide
Look at us—we've mastered it
The grand Electric Slide

Now here's to our instructor
She has taught us well
A toast, a cheer and kudos
For our own Glen Gal Belle

*

Adventures in PT
(Physical Therapy)

Once upon a time I fell and broke my wrist
It took me on a journey—one with quite a twist

First there's minor surgery—then there are the pins
At last we come to therapy and here's where fun begins

I walk into the center—music fills the air
Bells and bars and weights and stuff are spotted here and there

Broken bodies greet me limping round the room
It is a bit disheartening with a dreadful sense of gloom

First they heat your hand—and they freeze it too
I have to go along with it—what else am I to do?

Someone yanks my arm; someone gives me toys
I'm not in the mood to play—I make a lot of noise

Time goes by—I'm noticing—I start to use my hand
Wow! It must be working—I'm set to beat the band

Thanks to those who helped me—I know I raised some cane
And now I do apologize for being such a pain

*

My Purple Balloon

Mommy, mommy
I love it so
My purple balloon
You let it go

I love its color
I love its style
It makes me happy
It makes me smile

You let it go
And fly so high
It blew away
Up to the sky

My purple balloon
It was such fun
Mommy, mommy
You owe me one

Love,
Erin (Age 5)

*

Where Have All the Dummies Gone

Where have all the dummies gone?
Is it really so?
We walk among geniuses
No matter where we go

'See my son the doctor
My daughter passed the Bar'
Bravos echo far and wide
Everyone's a star

When it comes to grandkids
No one gets a 'B'
All are straight 'A' students
No mediocrity

Here comes that yearly letter
When greetings come to town
Oh if I could only hear
'Johnny is class clown'

Where have all the workers gone?
Those who pulled their weight
With pride in jobs well done
Those who made us great

Ponder this—an edifice
Designed by Frank Lloyd Wright
Sitting on the drawing board
But never brought to light

*

Food for Thought

Words

In the beginning was a 'word'
A sound—a grunt—a sigh
A way to say 'hello'
Or perhaps 'goodbye'

In time new words took shape
While eons slipped away
New meanings—new expressions
Evolving still today

Words can make you laugh
Words can make you cry
Words can make you smile
With a twinkle in your eye

Words that ring in eloquence
Can lead the flock astray
While compromising truth
They steal sweet souls away

Words can toll for peace
Or echo drums of war
Words can breed a grudge
That lingers ever more

Beyond that primal voice
Language grew and grew
Today—the sweetest words
A lilting 'I love you'

*

Footprints

Footprints in the sand
Footprints in the snow
Footprints set in cement
Those of long ago

In the course of time
Some will wash away
Others will remain
Forever and a day

With every step we take
Things we say and do
May leave a lasting memory
Or touch a heart or two

Behold a glowing image
In the windows of your mind
People warmly touched
By footprints left behind

*

Heroes

An image of a hero
Bursting through a burning door
Will stay with you forever
And yet there's something more

There are heroes we don't notice
As they go about their day
Giving of themselves
In a very different way

Folks who open heart and home
And take in as their own
Those with special needs
Or those who are alone

Caregivers in the shadows
Play a noble role
While tending to another
They give with heart and soul

Note heroes in our history books
Worthy of acclaim
Schindler with his epic list
And Miep of Anne Frank fame

Applaud the movie star
Cheer the baseball great
But hail the silent hero
And let it resonate

*

The Media

Hear Ye! Hear Ye! One and All
'Daytime follows night'
No two ways about it
Behold the dawning light

O hear the networks chant
"We tend to disagree
'Nighttime follows day'
Impartial, we must be"

May networks stand by facts
Not create confusion
Present the news with clarity
That defies illusion

Here and there a network
With a point of view
'Fair and Balanced'—Really?
I have a bridge for you

May broadcasts be free of spin
Where truth begins to flower
Broadcasts free of influence
Where money can't buy power

Hear Ye! Hear Ye! One and all
The news from A to Z
Truth shall echo far and wide
From sea to shining sea

*

The Wheel

Many roads lead to 'God'
Journeys far and wide
In churches, mosques and temples
Or a feeling deep inside

Like the spokes of a wheel
Converging at the core
The roads lead to a lofty place
Behold heaven's door

The roads are never shrouded
In ideology
But gleam in golden sunshine
For sweet humanity

Tis written in the wind
A prayer along the way
May peace embrace the earth
Forever and a day

*

Sweet Dreams

Cherish nature's gifts in life
Its wrath is set aside
Savor pleasant images
Sweetly let them glide

In the quiet of the night
When moonlight is agleam
Surrender to sweet slumber
Of rolling pastures, dream

Dream of waves that kiss the shore
And birds that fly on high
Behold mountain shadows
From peaks that touch the sky

As waters sing a rippling tune
The river makes its run
Now slowly drift to slumber land
Until the morning sun

*

Timing

Tis written in the stars
The book of destiny
Que sera, sera
What will be, will be

But timing plays a role
Along the road we take
When and where we go
Choices that we make

Oh—to time it right
Meet that special one
Find that perfect dream job
Where work is more like fun

Oh—to sell that stock
When the market's on the rise
And never see a nest egg
Vanish from one's eyes

Women's vote; Civil Rights
Progress sometimes waits
When overdue dreams come true
The nation celebrates

Timing plays a role
In destiny's embrace
We long for lucky stars
Right time! Right place!

*

Charisma

The power of charisma
Its mystery and lure
Can change the face of history
And evermore endure

Despots with charisma
Can lead the world astray
And those with sweet charisma
Can steal your heart away

What makes a Frank Sinatra?
Or a Marilyn Monroe?
Folks with much more talent
Would really like to know

A charismatic figure
A tongue sharp as a blade
Can lure the many followers
That's how cults are made

If only we could bottle it
Charisma for the good
To make this world a better place
If we only could

*

Culture Power

When I was a young girl
My mother said to me
A daughter is a burden
On the family

There isn't much for her to do
Until she finds a man
The thing to do is marry
As early as she can

My mother wasn't out of touch
That's all she ever knew
The culture of the day declared
What she believed was true

Society wields power
As in my mother's day
In all the cultures of the world
One bows to public sway

*

Change

As you travel through the years
Whatever fills your day
Do not fear the face of change
No matter come what may

When you are set in your ways
When your world is status quo
Think of joys you may have missed
And those you'll never know

Life is ever changing
And will forevermore
The best rewards may yet to be
Just beyond that door

In a portrait of a life
In this awesome fleeting game
Where change has been the option
Color fills the frame

*

Pollyanna Land

Once upon a time
In Pollyanna Land
People lived in harmony
How wonderful—how grand

In every little home
O hear a song of love
Echoing sweet tenderness
A blessing from above

In Pollyanna Land
A neighbor is a friend
Loyal, tried and true
With a helping hand to lend

And citizens take note
Wherever you may dwell
Leaders act with honor
They serve the people well

Hear Ye! Hear Ye! One and all
In Pollyanna World
United Nations keep the peace
Behold the flags unfurled

May Pollyanna dreams come true
Mid smiles and joy and laughter
May everyone beneath the sun
Live happily ever after

*

Frustration

To lie in bed and sleep not
The night will never end
To toss and turn the whole night through
When sleep does not befriend

To wait for one who comes not
And gaze upon the door
To listen for those footsteps
Whose face you see no more

To try to please and please not
Response is a rebuff
Try this and that and everything
It's never quite enough

Some of life's frustrations
May wound a weary soul
But peace will come another day
And make the spirit whole

*

Forgiveness

There's a weight upon your shoulder
You've carried it too long
Life presents a downside
When someone's done you wrong

You go about your day
But something's not quite right
You cannot put your finger on
An ache that's out of sight

Apologies are welcome
But to your heart be true
It's not the one who's done you wrong
The answer rests with you

The power of forgiveness
Can lift the mighty weight
Letting go the burden
Brings peace—we celebrate

A message to remember
Hear ye! Toll the bell
To err is human—a fact of life
Forgive yourself as well

*

Vessels

A vessel that holds hatred
Destroys itself in time
It robs itself of precious years
In a deadly paradigm

And so it is with anger, pride
And greed and jealousy
And vengeance is a mighty force
That saps the energy

The vessel has so little room
For harmony and peace
So little room for confidence
That makes self-worth increase

A heart that casts the demons out
Rids itself of strife
And opens up to lasting love
The greatest gift in life

*

Looking Down

Imagine there's an alien
Looking down on earth
What would he be thinking
As he scanned its girth

Would he be puzzled
Would he laugh or would he cry
Would he be amused
Or would he ask 'why?'

What would he be thinking
Of jealousy and pride
While illness, pain and suffering
Echoed far and wide

As he witnessed conflict
Inhumane and cruel
Would he think that madness
Was the golden rule

And as he searched for happiness
Would he begin to doubt
Would he ask the question
'What's it all about?'

*

Why

If I had the power
To see earth from the sky
I'd look for signs of meaning
Of this and that and why

I'd look for signs of sunshine
For laughter and sweet smiles
But then I'd see the storm clouds
Embracing many miles

I'd look for signs of joy
In pockets far and wide
Of little bits of happiness
That warm the soul inside

Is peace and contentment
For just a random few?
Is joy a passing pleasure
Ever to pursue?

After all that comes to pass
No matter who we are
Are we just a tiny speck
Underneath a star?

*

Poignant Moments

It's so sad to see
A marriage fall apart
Hopes and dreams go up in smoke
Behold a broken heart

It's so sad to see
A grudge that's held too long
The reason—long forgotten
What had gone so wrong?

It's so sad to see
A child who waits for Dad
When wait is all she ever does
Indeed it's very sad

It's so sad to see
An old man all alone
With great anticipation
That a loved-one would phone

It's so sad to realize
Well-meaning souls abound
Wrapped in human nature's flaws
That echo all around

Poignant moments touch all lives
Life can't be all fun
We come out stronger in the end
When all is said and done

*

Womanizer

To spend a life of conquest
A drive to have one more
No matter who the woman is
The next one through the door

Precious time spent chasing
And playing cunning games
Master of deception
For those who have no names

For pleasure of the moment
A heavy price is paid
The price is never knowing
The sacrifices made

To miss the joy of loving
Emotions set in ice
Lasting unions not to be
What greater sacrifice

*

The One Commandment

One commandment says it all
A thought to keep in mind
Let it fill your heart
It is—Thou shalt be kind

If everyone around the world
Would honor this today
The evil that surrounds us
Perhaps would melt away

Think of the commandments
Take them from the start
It would be hard to break them
If kindness filled your heart

Not an easy task
We're human after all
No matter how we try
We may sometimes fall

In the journey of life
No matter what we find
Remember the commandment
It is—Thou shalt be kind

*

Consolation

A baby in its mother's womb
Of birth would be afraid
To leave the only world it's known
Would be an awesome trade

But after birth the babe would find
Itself in love's embrace
Showered with affection
Beneath a smiling face

Surely now the child would say
"Why did I fear so much?
These are loving arms that hold
And tender to the touch"

Life to death is really birth
Where souls will now awaken
Into a new and better world
Life is changed, not taken

Those left behind should not despair
As though all hope were gone
Today and when we join them
Our dear ones do live on

*

Seasons

Seasons

Trees grow lush with greenery
Birds begin to sing
Rains bring forth the flowers
These are joys of spring

Skies embrace a rainbow
Beyond a crackling storm
Golden days of summer
Are radiant and warm

Rejoice in brilliant colored leaves
In fall when winds will blow
They cling to trees in autumn
But then they must let go

Then winter's quiet falling snow
Boldly meets our door
And leaves a coat of beauty
Till spring is here once more

*

The Calendar

Winter perfect scenery
Glazed in ice and snow
Ringing in another year
While frosty breezes blow

Time to say, "I love you"
To those we hold dear
Loud enough to resonate
And last throughout the year

It enters like a lion
We celebrate Saint Pat
It exits like a little lamb
Along with this and that

Early spring—trees are bare
Jokes on fools are played
Rains bring forth the greenery
While prints of winter fade

We remember mama
For all that she has done
We honor all our heroes
They gave for everyone

We remember papa
We celebrate our dads
Congratulations granted
To the newest grads

The Star Spangled Banner
Independence Day
Marching bands beat the drums
On Main Street, USA

Dog-days of summer
A rumbling thunder shower
Cicadas rule the night
As they chirp away each hour

Yellow buses everywhere
Off to school they go
The autumnal equinox
How the seasons flow

Days drenched in color
Falling leaves of gold
Gremlins, ghosts and goblins lurk
Scary stories told

Frost is on the pumpkin
Lofty trees are bare
Turkey in the oven
Family everywhere

Deck the Halls! Toll the Bells!
May peace embrace the land
Echoing Good Will
With people hand in hand

*

A Roller Coaster in the Sea

A roller coaster in the sea
An image to behold
Nature on a rampage
Tragic stories told

Now the rolling ocean waves
Gently kiss the shore
The storm is part of history
Its roar is heard no more

Twas once a great attraction
A lofty, awesome ride
Gleeful screams would fill the air
And echo far and wide

Memories of a boardwalk
Where childhood dreams come true
Memories of a sandy beach
Beneath a sky of blue

Reflections of sweet yesterday
Visions of 'back when'
The shore in all its glory
Shall return again

A roller coaster in the sea
A symbol to be sure
Despite the wrath of nature
The spirit shall endure

*

Between the Raindrops

Walk between the raindrops
On a rainy day
It may cheer you up
And chase the blues away

I'll not bemoan the fact
That I can't see the sun
A golden moment may unfold
Before the day is done

I met a couple as I walked
Along the road one day
We exchanged sweet greetings
Then ambled on our way

Soon the sky turned dark
And rain began to fall
"I'll hurry home," I thought
"I'll not get wet at all"

But rain, it did—and just ahead
The couple, plain to see
Holding an umbrella
They offered it to me

It may seem insignificant
A simple thing to do
To me—a golden moment
The sun is shining through

*

March

It comes in like a lion
Mid freezing ice and snow
The grip of old man winter
Not ready to let go

Days beat on in cadence
The ides of March grow near
We celebrate Saint Pat
O hear the Irish cheer

The vernal equinox
When daylight equals night
A sign that winter's almost done
To everyone's delight

In the rhythm of the seasons
A weather pattern weaves
One day cold; the next day warm
And like a lamb—it leaves

*

Henry's Garden

When Henry was a young lad
During World War II
He kept a tidy garden
It was the thing to do

'Victory Gardens' rose
All across the land
A nation united
Americans hand in hand

When the war was won
Beyond the roaring cheers
Henry had a hobby
To last for many years

He learned to love the soil
And watch the seedlings grow
Tomatoes, peas, asparagus
Neatly in a row

His hobby served him well
With each passing day
When life seemed somewhat tough
It chased the blues away

While time beats on in cadence
And seasons ever flow
The garden holds sweet memories
Of a lad from long ago

*

Dog Days of Summer

Dog days of summer
Ball games, picnics, fun
Friends and family revel
In the blazing sun

A rumbling thunder storm
Crackling through the heat
Ushers in a weather change
A breath of air—how sweet

Evenings bring the creatures out
Cicadas rule the night
Chirping through each hour
Until the dawning light

Days begin to dwindle
Shadows grow long
Signs of what lies ahead
O hear the autumn song

*

Yellow Buses

Yellow buses everywhere
Back to school they go
Time for new beginnings
Time to learn and grow

Clamor fills the air
Bullies acting tough
Anxious little five-year olds
Backpacks, books and stuff

Little do they realize
They're building memories
Of reading, writing, 'rithmetic
And learning ABC's

Images of schooldays
Moments to remember
Yellow buses dot the land
On a day in September

*

Autumn

Autumn takes the stage
In a classic, timeless show
Nature paints a masterpiece
With images aglow

Days drenched in color
Winds caress the trees
Leaves begin to tumble
Rippling in the breeze

Gremlins, ghosts and goblins lurk
By Jack-O-Lantern's light
Haunted houses wail
Through the spooky night

Frost is on the pumpkin
Turkey time draws near
When families celebrate their gifts
For another year

Images to savor
As time consumes the fall
Before the winter snows
And autumn's curtain call

*

Ice Dance

Winter's crystal tapestry
More treacherous than snow
Displays its glacial presence
With icing all aglow

Behold dancing cars
Spinning round and round
And lofty, mighty power lines
Falling to the ground

Trees with clinging, frosty coats
Wildly bend and sway
And shattering glass will fall to earth
When heavy ice gives way

Broken diamonds all around
Crunch beneath your feet
You slip and slide in your attempt
To cross the icy sheet

Scenes of winter magic
Of beauty to behold
Belie its cunning nature
Forbidding, stark and cold

Twinkling rays of sunshine
Sparkle and beguile
Through crystal covered tree tops
For just a little while

But as in all the winters past
The ice will melt away
With promise for tomorrow
Of a warm and golden day

*

The Babbling Brook

O hear the Babbling Brook
What stories does it tell?
Of history, of people
Of rains when waters swell?

Hear its age old song
What secrets does it hold?
Does it note sweet voices
As young lovers' dreams unfold?

Behold rippling waters
On a golden summer day
That weave through ice in winter
While seasons slip away

It trickles on in cadence
And echoes through the years
Listen to the melody
It's music to the ears

Gaze upon the waters
Let the melody resound
Feel a sense of peace
Savor sight and sound

The waters skip across the stones
In a rhythmic, timeless dance
O hear the Babbling Brook
A song of sweet romance

*

The Lake

Sunrise at the lake
A new day has begun
As in many days before
Beneath a golden sun

The lake—embraced by seasons
When seeds are sown in spring
When raindrops dot the waters
And lilting birds take wing

The lake—embraced by summer
When friendly people meet
And children romp along the shore
A picture—oh so sweet

The lake—embraced by autumn
When days are drenched in gold
When leaves begin to tumble
And brilliant scenes unfold

And then in winter's full embrace
With sheets of ice and snow
Skaters glide across the ice
Weaving to and fro

Behold the setting sun
That gleams from shore to shore
Then sinks beneath the sky
Till morning dawns once more

*

The Weather

I love the golden sunshine
And too I love the rain
I love when snowflakes softly
Caress my windowpane

I love when winds propel the leaves
Round and round they swirl
When days are drenched in color
And rippling flags unfurl

But on the other hand
I do not like the sleet
And most all in summer
I do not like the heat

Weather rules the day
Nothing we can do
Behold a fluffy rain cloud
And then a sky of blue

*

Thanksgiving

A Norman Rockwell painting
Speaks volumes of the day
Of family and blessings
More than words can say

When I see the painting
I think of history
I think about the Pilgrims
They dared to cross the sea

With stark determination
They faced the great unknown
Through hardship and adversity
While freedom seeds were sown

These hearty seeds took root
Mid struggles and mid tears
And blossomed for the people
Lo these many years

I see the Pilgrims in my mind
Together hand in hand
Giving thanks and praise
For the blessings of this land

Then I see the painting
Hanging on the wall
No need to say a word
The painting says it all

*

Holidays

Magic Moment
(A Christmas Story)

Twas Christmas Eve some years ago / A snowstorm came along
Behold a winter wonderland / O hear a Yuletide song

We couldn't get the car out / It was buried in the snow
With one more gift yet to buy / The sky was getting low

I asked my daughter Karen / A girl of nine or ten
If she would like to walk to town / For shopping once again

We set out, just the two of us / Dressed from head to toe
Our boots made prints beneath our feet / Crunching in the snow

This was a happy time for me / Sharing with my girl
A moment of her childhood / She was my little pearl

We reached a winding in the road / And started down the hill
Darkness fell upon us / And winter's frosty chill

We saw a pretty little house / Where twinkling colors glowed
The house was nestled in the woods / With trees along the road

The trees were dressed in ice and snow / A magic moment made
The sight we were about to see / We wished would never fade

Dazzling lights from the house / Pierced the icy trees
And danced like sparkling colored jewels / Suspended in the breeze

A symphony of color / A symphony of light
Splendor filled the air / On this holy night

We stood there, the two of us / Enraptured and in awe
My baby and me / A miracle, we saw

The magic of the moment / Born of ice and snow
Remains a joyous memory / Of Christmas long ago
*

A Village Christmas

Deck the Halls with boughs of holly
Hark the Yuletide bell
Tis Christmas in our village
Where good neighbors dwell

Hear the carols resonate
And Jingle Bells ring
O Little Town of Bethlehem
Hear the people sing

A Symphony of Christmas
Splendor fills the air
With wishes for sweet blessings
An answer to a prayer

May peace embrace our village
And echo with our word
Let none of us in need of help
Call out and not be heard

May differences be small
This Silent, Holy Night
Let beacons of kindness
Be our guiding light

Joy to the World
Let it begin right here
May peace and love abound
And last throughout the year

*

Christmas Song

Another year has slipped away
Into eternity
A year of poignant moments
We've shared as family

Behold the festival balloons
In times of celebration
Behold the warm embrace
In times of jubilation

We've had our awkward moments
We're human after all
But let us not forget
Our differences are small

O hear the carols resonate
Around the Christmas tree
Open up your heart for love
And ever let it be

*

Home Sweet Home

O Little town of Bethlehem / A village made in heaven
A lovely corner of the world / Made for Jody and Kevin

Nestled in the town / On a very pretty street
Sits a very pretty house / A picture oh so sweet

Here now, the holidays / A first Christmas tree
In the very pretty house / With friends and family

They open their door / With grace and style
To a home filled with warmth / And a welcoming smile

Hear the festive music / A lilting melody
Behold a lovely miss / That's Killian you see

And prancing all around / Or curled up in a chair
Is a furry little butterball / It's Sadye everywhere

Those of us who love them / Who hold them dear
Wish that love grows sweeter / With every passing year

May golden moments fill this home / As precious days unfold
And echo with sweet memories / To cherish and to hold

Love, Grandma Chrissy

*

Festive Holidays

Once again a year has passed
Into infinity
A year of golden moments
Etched in memory

And now the carols resonate
Sweet music fills the air
Trees are twinkling all about
Magic everywhere

May peace and love and joy
Last throughout the year
Savor every warm embrace
Savor all the cheer

Enjoy the folks around you
This festive holiday
Enjoy the moment here and now
Before it slips away

*

Christmas a l'Alus

Twas the week before Christmas when all through the Glen
Folks were ready to party again

The kittens were nestled all snug in their hutch
While purring and dreaming of catnip and such

We're met at the door with a nod and a wink
"Come in," says Mike, "What will you drink?"

They open their home with grace and style
We're greeted by Dorian with an elegant smile

When what to our wondering eyes should appear
But a dazzling tree in a room full of cheer

Tis Holiday Time; Tis Christmas once more
With feelings of warmth and blessings galore

Then up to his feet jumps John with a song
We all tap our toes; we all sing along

How lucky are we to be among friends
On a night full of joy that we wish never ends

But then in a twinkling the evening is through
Thanks for new memories to a pair named Alu

I heard them exclaim as we strode out of sight
"Happy Christmas to all and to all a good night"

Christmas 2006

Tis the Season

Tis the season for good will
To echo round the world
A time for peace on earth
Mid rippling flags unfurled

Tis the season to embrace
Those we hold dear
And cherish precious memories
We've made throughout the year

Tis the season to resolve
In the year ahead
To open up our hearts
Wherever we may tread

Tis the season to give thanks
For blessings from above
The sweetest one of all
This noble thing called love

*

A Christmas Wish

Christmas is for peace and joy
And love and happiness
Christmas is for dreams come true
And loved ones to caress

Christmas is a time
For cheer and mistletoe
A time to toast a gracious heart
Where sweet blessings flow

If I had the power
To bestow these gifts on you
I'd sprinkle you with blessings
To last the whole year through

And when the year is over
Remember now and then
I'd get my magic sprinkles
And I'd do it all again

*

Christmas Greetings

*

Christmas time has come to pass
With gifts and mistletoe
The greatest gift of all in life
For love to grow and grow
**

Christmas is a rhapsody
Ringing from the soul
Two hearts beat ever closer
As Christmas bells toll
**

A season to remember
The greatest gift to give
This noble gift that we call love
For love is why we live
**

Twas the night before Christmas
A year has gone by
We add to our memories
Our love will not die
**

May peace and love and blessings
Embraced by mistletoe
Warm you deep inside
And set your heart aglow
**

My Travels

My Dentist

Twice a year for many years / I've climbed into the chair
To hold on to my pearly whites / Through years of wear and tear

My dentist makes it interesting / He talks and talks and talks
Of this and that and everything / Around the chair he walks

It never fails to happen / My finest thoughts are when
My mouth is full of hands and tools / Foiled once again

One day I made a visit / And soon he said to me
"How was your vacation?" / And then, "What did you see?"

I thought and thought and thought / It proved to be a chore
At last he caught my eye and said / "What are you waiting for?"

I promised then and there / That I would take a trip
Before my next appointment / By plane or train or ship

"A promise is a promise" / I repeated to myself
Besides, I never want to find / My teeth upon a shelf

So off I went to see the world / I crossed the briny sea
I saw the Changing of the Guard / Rome and Gay Paree

On a wild safari / O hear the lions roar
Behold the Incan treasures / The Kremlin and more

I've traveled far and wide / I'll have so much to say
When next my dentist asks / "How was your holiday?"

*

171

Adventures of Glen Gals
(The Balkans)

We set out on a journey
My buddies and me
Glen Gals venture forth
In camaraderie

There's Annie with her Irish brogue
Mary loves to chat
Rose will tell it like it is
And then there's our pal Pat

My traveling companions
We're off to see the world
In search of diverse cultures
Behold the flags unfurled

We headed for a region
On the Adriatic Sea
A group of new Republics
Learning to be free

Euros, kunas, dollars
How will we keep it straight
Echoes of a foreign tongue
Broadly resonate

We had a bunch of laughs
Amid the oohs and aahs
And in the square a four piece band
O hear the oom pah pahs

We walked along the water
An aura filled the air
Mystic sounds encircled us
And echoed everywhere

With every step we took
An eerie melody
The tide would lash against the pipes
Of the organ by the sea

Autumn's mountain shadows fall
Across the roofs of slate
Winter pays a visit
And vistas radiate

Let's not forget the people
All across the land
'Hvala! Dobro Jutro!'
Prepared to lend a hand

When next somebody asks
'Why go so far away?'
I'll smile with satisfaction
I'll have a lot to say

Glen Gals heading home
To our beloved shore
'To see the world', Jefferson said
'Is to love America more'

*

The Night Before Christmas
(In Antarctica)

Twas the night before Christmas
And all through the ship
Not a creature was stirring
On this wondrous trip

We passengers settled
All snug in our bunk
Completely surrounded
By all of our junk

While visions of penguins
Danced in our head
Andrew was plotting
We had nothing to dread

Waves began swirling
Up and then down
Our stomachs were churning
And churning around

The Russians are coming
So cheery and bright
Their smiles are radiant
A perfect delight

And then in a twinkling
It's time to get dressed
With layers of clothing
Topped by our vest

Now up to the deck top
We're going to sea
Climb into the Zodiac
And don't forget me

Our vessel sailed on
In magic delight
Through icebergs that sparkled
In blue and in white

Explorers are we
With fervor and pep
Looking for penguins
Just watch where you step

When what to our wondering
Eyes should appear?
But a humpback whale
Surprisingly near

Now Russian, now Spanish
Now English, now French
What could they be saying
What means this word "mensch"?

We'll speak not a word
Except if it's good
We'll love one another
The way that we could

May echoes of peace
And love from the heart
Be carried away
As passengers part

And I heard from the ship
As it sailed out of sight
"Happy Christmas to all
And to all a good night"

*

175

Across the Pond

Parlate inglese? Sprechen Sie englisch? / Parlez-vous anglais?
Does anyone speak English? / Is what we're trying to say

It helps to know the language / In travels far and wide
In Italy and Switzerland / And France's countryside

Mary asks the questions / For answers we have Rose
Annie holds the Euros / The language—no one knows

The culture of Milan / Fills us with delight
Fashion, art and music / Culture left and right

Majestic mountains radiate / Embraced by Alps are we
Inside the rocking cable car / Mid breathless scenery

Clickity clack—clickity clack / We ride the speedy train
We're off to Gay Paree / Along the River Seine

Behold the Eiffel Tower / Reaching for the sky
The Louvre and Notre Dame / Snapshots catch our eye

History holds epic tales / That make a nation weep
We walk the beach of Omaha / Where young heroes sleep

In poignancy we travel on / Our journey near an end
The stage is set for heading home / To family and friend

Enter—weary travelers / Weary through and through
On to our America / O hear—Merci beaucoup

*

Iceland

Faces of travelers / Were eager and bright
Set for adventure / Ready for flight

A welcome in Reykjavik / When flying was done
Behold weary travelers / Scant was the sun

We stepped into darkness / And got on the bus
And then right on cue / Snow greeted us

We drove through the night / As flakes cast a spell
An eerie ride / To reach our hotel

No matter how tired / We were ready to tour
To see grand attractions / This country has lure

The people are friendly / English we hear
With hardly an accent / Articulate—clear

We toured lava fields / More memories to keep
We saw many horses / And many more sheep

We then took a dip / In the Blue Lagoon
Hot Springs around us / It ended too soon

Goodbye fishing village / And tectonic plate
Goodbye faithful geysers / Our home lies in wait

*

A Scandinavian Odyssey

Glaciers forged a masterpiece that stands in majesty
Norsemen filled the history books—they dared to cross the sea

Land of fishing villages and streets of cobblestones
Where sovereigns ruled the populace from their lofty thrones

Land of changing boundaries of Finns and Danes and Swedes
Divided by an unseen line yet born of Nordic seeds

While time consumed the ages mid wars and kings and queens
Changing ever slowly—changing were the scenes

Fast forward to a different world where multi-cultures dwell
Where tourists dot the landscape in search of tales to tell

Enter—weary travelers with Lars to lead the way
Excellent is he—we shall not go astray

Magic moments resonate with one of our rewards
The panoramic splendor of the magnificent fjords

History and culture, the Nobel Prize
Visions to remember rose before our eyes

Too soon the tour was over—good-byes would fill the air
We had become a family—sweet sadness everywhere

We came from every region, from sea to shining sea
O beautiful America—we're heading home to thee

*

Paris

We span the great Atlantic / We're off to Gay Paree
Three ladies from America / Anne, Kristine and Bea

The lofty Eiffel Tower / So vibrant and alive
Counts days till the millennium / Six hundred eighty-five

Behold the Arc de Triomphe / With awesome majesty
The flame that burns for heroes / For all eternity

We buy the metro tickets / No simple thing to do
Amid the great confusion / A sweet 'merci beaucoup'

Crowds queue up in sheer delight / To sail upon the Seine
French is ringing in our ears / From every gal and swain

We tour the famous Louvre / And Notre Dame in awe
The Palace at Versailles / Another tourist draw

Among attractions of the world / France has played a role
Its gift to us, Miss Liberty / New York City's soul

Soon it's time to say goodbye / To France our gracious host
On to our America / The land we love the most

February, 1998

*

179

Greece

I cross the Great Atlantic—I'm on my way to Greece
In search of ancient cultures where wonders never cease

I find the world of Byzantine with icons flecked with gold
And many wondrous artifacts—a chalice to behold

Beneath the earth a city sleeps at least a thousand years
Until one day it comes to pass—an ancient world appears

And then a highlight of my quest that I would never miss
I climb the mighty endless steps to the Acropolis

The pillars stand in majesty—a thrill to gaze upon
Splendor from the past—the golden Parthenon

The Stadium Olympia—five rings speak good will
A rippling flag against the sky makes my heart stand still

Let's not forget the islands that Greece is famous for
Patmos, Rhodes and Mykonos and many, many more

Their beauty is exquisite, from the ship we view
Isles with whitewashed houses framed by skies of blue

I see the blue-green waters; we're reaching for the sky
Cotton clouds beneath my wings as we say 'goodbye'

There is below my window a disappearing coast
On to my America the land I love the most

*

Egypt

Once upon a culture / In a land of mystic style
A wealth of ancient treasures / Embraced the River Nile

While time consumed the centuries / And years passed by the score
Entombed and still and silent / Lay artifacts galore

In time the age-old mysteries / Began to stir in sleep
With echoes of antiquity / Rising from the deep

Hieroglyphics blazoned / Sweet secrets would unfold
With relics from the ruins / And artifacts of gold

Silhouettes of Pyramids / Adorn a painted sky
While mystic, enigmatic Sphinx / And Obelisks reach high

Fire of the blazing sun / Tracks the mighty Nile
And camels cross the desert / In tandem mile by mile

From temples of antiquity / Anthems fill the air
With echoes of the faithful / In symphony of prayer

Pageantry of Egypt / Glorious and vast
Proclaims its wealth of history / Awakened from the past

*

South Africa

We landed in Johannesburg from places far and wide
Stepping into Africa, agog and starry-eyed

We ventured into Kruger Park—our fervor persevered
While seeking native animals that suddenly appeared

First we saw a lion and then a fine giraffe
Wild exotic animals we loved to photograph

Kudus, gnus and rhinos, impalas everywhere
Performed before enraptured eyes, the dance extraordinaire

Then someone saw an elephant, first one, then two, then three
Before our eyes the numbers grew into infinity

There is a place called Swaziland, a kingdom we passed through
It sounds to me like make-believe where happy dreams come true

Zulus entertained us—the women wore no top
The men were so enjoying it, I thought their eyes would pop

One more jewel of Africa before we cross the sea
Capetown so magnificent, one more memory

Majestic Table Mountain—the city at its feet
Breathless gorgeous scenery where mighty oceans meet

Soon the words were spoken, 'Goodbye and keep in touch
Though we may never meet again, I'm glad we shared so much'

*

India

Imagine a culture different from your own
People live in poverty—it's all they've ever known

A land of cycles, cars and carts and mass humanity
Where creatures roam the villages and cows trod lazily

Camels dot the picture pulling heavy loads
Rickshaws prance in tandem along the dusty roads

Grandeur of temples revered with unshod feet
Hovels and beggars—men peeing in the street

Atop the lofty elephant mid giggles, glee and fuss
We bounce along the cobblestones with monkeys watching us

We tour with mixed emotions, joyous at the start
Till pleas from wide eyed children are tugging at your heart

Memories of India with visions to recall
A land of contradictions that boasts the Taj Mahal

Scenes beneath my window grow small and disappear
En route to my America, the land I hold so dear

*

China

Chronicles of China for many centuries
Were manifest in emperors and mighty dynasties

Forbidden City sagas, palaces and things
The sound of plinking instruments—Chinese music rings

Where once the tribal sentries trod, there lives a legacy
A mighty fortress stands aloft in timeless majesty

A land where once tradition held that women bind their feet
Where baby boys were worshipped and girls were bittersweet

When revolution swept the land in nineteen forty nine
The open market lost its breath by government design

People grew in numbers exponentially and wild
The time had come for families to settle for one child

Change embraced the century—upheaval here and there
Signs of history at work on Tiananmen Square

Then something was unfolding for all the world to see
Beijing started marching to a world economy

A symphony of changing times echoes round the world
As China struts to rock and roll with banners now unfurled

With all the changes taking place, if he were here today
"Love and kindness shall prevail," oh hear Confucius say

*

Peru

The Andes hold a treasure, incredible but true
Brilliant Incan Culture—the jewel of Peru

Adventure fills the air as we bubble with delight
Sixteen sprightly travelers eager to take flight

Marisella is our tour guide—she slowly leads the way
Our protector and our lecturer, we shall not go astray

A Quechuan village luncheon with a native family
We see Chinchero women weaving skillfully

The people live so simply in colorful attire
In houses made of mud with little they desire

We hike the narrow pathways where the air is thin
Amid the gorgeous vistas with breathless joy within

We float upon the waters of the Urubamba River
The calm and then the rush make the spirit quiver

Mystic Machu Picchu is at my fingertip
Ancient architecture, the highlight of the trip

The aura of the countryside, its color, mud-brick brown
Is different in its character from any that we found

Too soon the tour is over; 'Goodbyes' were soon to be
There was a touch of sadness—we were a family

*

The Pompous Tour
(The Pampas)

I went to Argentina
To see what I could see
I heard about the 'Pompous Tour'
And said, "Wow, that's for me"

We rode upon the Pompous Bus
Our noses in the air
Strutting up and down the aisle
An answer to a prayer

We reached our destination
Our spirits flying high
We bumped into each other
Chins pointing to the sky

In quest of grandiosity
The finest in our class
A man of great pomposity
Fell upon his ass

And then the tour was over
Our noses back in place
Time to taste some humble pie
A pie right in your face

Memories of pompous times
Ring clearly as a bell
I recall the pompous fall
I learned my lesson well

*

A Ribbon in the Sky

My weary head was resting on the windowpane
Flying halfway round the world and eager to deplane

The sky outside my window was very black indeed
Except for twinkling diamonds not ready to recede

Suddenly I noticed from the corner of my eye
Across the broad horizon, a ribbon in the sky

A long slim line of radiance—a brilliant scarlet red
I'd never seen a sight like this—I raised my weary head

My gaze was fixed to keep in view this royal masterpiece
And savor every moment as magic would increase

I watched the line grow wider—my eyes were kept on track
The ribbon turning orange—the sky was still pitch-black

Slowly it was changing and pink was now the hue
As the diamonds faded, the sky was turning blue

The stage was yet evolving in a timeless cosmic dance
A golden arc was rising across the grand expanse

And then the tempo quickened in a splendid symphony
Crescendo building to a peak with awe and majesty

I felt a surge of music as I witnessed waning night
Then cymbals pierced the heavens heralding dawn's light

SUNRISE
*

America

Old Glory

I love to see Old Glory
Flap nobly as winds blow
With brilliant red, royal blue
And white as driven snow

Red is blood of patriots
Blue is loyalty
White is pureness of intent
Old Glory waves for thee

It symbolizes liberty
Opportunity for all
A land where freedom echoes
From Independence Hall

Ever does this banner fly
In brilliance coast to coast
It is a mighty symbol
That people matter most

*

My Album of America

From the Great Atlantic Ocean
To the Pacific far away
Snapshots of the land I love
The good old USA

Behold Acadia National Park
Where grandeur meets the sea
Where first light greets America
And spans on endlessly

The Grand Niagara Falls
Gushing forth in thunder
Cascading through the centuries
Epitome of wonder

Icons etched in stone
Framed in majesty
Mount Rushmore on display
For posterity

Bubbling springs at Yellowstone
Old Faithful does her thing
Bison, moose and grizzlies
And birds upon the wing

Fishermen's Wharf in Frisco
The famous Golden Gate
Chinatown and Cable Cars
The street that is not straight

The glitter of Las Vegas
Sparkle fills the air
Blinking, pulsing colored lights
Neon everywhere

Waters carved a masterpiece
That endures today
Massive, epic canyon walls
Take your breath away

Mardi Gras in New Orleans
Where soulful jazz was born
See the marching minstrel man
As he blows his horn

Behold The Magic Kingdom
Where children's dreams come true
Mickey Mouse and scary rides
So many things to do

A National Park like Yellowstone
Except no bubbling springs
Animals and woods and streams
And peaks with smoky rings

Visions of our Capitol
Washington, DC
Memorials and monuments
Bespeak Democracy

At last—the awesome Lady
Who holds a torch on high
In tribute to the oceans crossed
For dreams that touch the sky

Oohs and ahs echo
As the album's put away
Snapshots held in my heart
For another day

*

Dreams of Our Founders

Government of the people
O hear our founders say
Not only of the privileged
Of everyone, said they

Government by the people
O hear our founders say
Not only by the powerful
By real folks holding sway

Government for the people
O hear our founders say
Not only for the few
For the masses come what may

Of and by and for
A noble resume
A land embraced by justice
O hail the USA

*

The Constitution

'We the people' resonates
And echoes through the years
To form a perfect union
O hail our pioneers

Establish justice through the land
Insure tranquility
Provide for the common defense
In our democracy

Promote the general welfare
A decent life for all
Along with blessed liberty
Tis written on the wall

Justice, peace and welfare
It is plain to see
Our Founders' lofty goal
For sweet humanity

When all is said and done
A preamble, well versed
A message of hope
The people shall come first

*

A Perfect Union

To form a perfect Union
Our Founders' lofty goal
They strove to get it right
They played a noble role

There was no way of knowing
What challenges they'd meet
The baby nation struggled
To stand up on its feet

The young Republic grew
While crisis lay in store
Something had been festering
O hear the drums of war

The Union nearly crumbled
Divided was the land
But it was written in the wind
United it would stand

Fast forward to the Thirties
The Great Depression years
Mid deep despair the nation learned
To conquer fruitless fears

Meanwhile clouds were looming
Shadows crossed the sea
America was drawn to war
And stormed to victory

We the People shall survive
Whatever comes our way
A tribute to our Founders
O hail the USA

*

Land of the Free

A land free of poverty
O let it resonate
Elimination of the poor
O let us celebrate

A land that echoes fairness
Where everyone works hard
Dreaming of that little house
White pickets round the yard

A land free to carry on
In the shadow of defeat
Where a safety net can help folks
Get back on their feet

A land free of plutocrats
Who buy their way to power
A land free from spin
Where truth begins to flower

No need for pompous charity
From the mansions to the shacks
A land where no one ever
Falls between the cracks

A land free to reach a goal
Or chase a lofty dream
Opportunity for all
Where justice reigns supreme

*

Mosaic

Oh to see a world
Where 'different' is respected
Perhaps there would be fewer wars
Toward peace we'd be directed

A Mosaic is America
Not a melting pot
Pieces placed together
Dissolved, they were not

Different cultures bless us all
When we take what's right
Out of every walk of life
And bring it into light

Let's get to know each other
And let all talent show
Encourage creativity
For with it we all grow

*

A Golden Moment

A moment to remember
A page in history
America had spoken
From sea to shining sea

Tear drenched faces in the crowd
Hope embraced the day
A tribute to the brave souls
Who dared to pave the way

Rosa boldly held her seat
Others beat the drum
Martin spoke with eloquence
"We shall overcome"

"We hold these truths"
Echoes in the Hall
From Thomas Jefferson's pen
Equality for all

Lincoln's voice still resonates
From eighteen sixty three
"We shall not perish from the earth"
United States are we

A golden moment touched the hearts
Of people round the world
Old Glory reaches for the sky
Behold our flag unfurled

Tuesday
November 4, 2008
11:pm

*

199

The Republic

A Republic for People—what a noble endeavor
A glorious doctrine to last forever

People deserve government's best
A noble congress will honor this quest

A land of freedom and dreams come true
For all of its citizens and not just a few

For those down and out—give them a lift
Reward incentive and that is a gift

As Americans prosper and ride the good track
Is it not time to give something back?

Tax is not always a terrible thing
It is how it's used and what it can bring

Checks and balances—not to forget
Extremes in the spectrum—an insidious threat

Our sacred document—it is worthy to note
Once allowed slavery and denied women's vote

We cherish the words, writing sublime
That speak for justice and echo with time

Let us remember an American theme
A Republic for People—our forefather's dream

*

FDR

Cries for greatness trumpet when crucial times are spun
In founding our America, behold George Washington

And Lincoln kept our nation whole when some would break away
"We shall not perish from the earth," he said one fateful day

In nineteen hundred thirty two, locked in deep despair
Our nation longed for signs of hope through weary eyes and prayer

Then as fate would have it, FDR appears
He gave the people confidence—he took away their fears

They listened to his voice that echoed far and wide
They clung to every word he spoke from a glowing fireside

Meanwhile far across the sea, madmen were at work
Fascists and Communists—the world had gone berserk

Decisions faced our president so difficult to make
With calls for isolation and Democracy at stake

And while he faced each battle, many did not know
He waged a war with something else—the scourge called polio

He saved us from the "isms" that plagued the century
He bore the priceless gift of hope—his noble legacy

When all was said and done, his greatness had prevailed
Through trials and tribulations, to our chief we hailed

*

John Harlan

Plessy vs. Ferguson
The Court had had its say
'Separate but Equal'
The ruling of the day

The lone dissenting Justice
John Harlan was his name
Nestled in the history books
Of judiciary fame

It took some generations
For the world to see
His wisdom and his courage
Now we all agree

The voice of the majority
O hear the roaring crowd
It doesn't make it right
Just because it's loud

*

Two Schools

Two schools of thought
Striving to hold sway
'Free Markets work the best'
Oh hear some people say

But on the other hand
Some would disagree
A safety net is needed
In stark adversity

Peril lies in both extremes
At risk—Democracy
With 'laissez faire' the rich may rule
In sheer Plutocracy

And at the other end
Much too much control
Can crush an opportunity
To reach a lofty goal

A Party that allows
Extremes to hold power
History will remember
Tis not its finest hour

Two parties can work well
When they reach across the aisle
To make the world a better place
Make it all worthwhile

*

The Pendulum

The pendulum in motion
Back and forth it swings
From one end to the other
Mid hopes and dreams and things

In the culture of our world
At times it leaves the track
Off in one direction
O when will it swing back?

All across the land
People old and young
Feel the mighty power
The pendulum has swung

Perspective and opinion
A certain point of view
Balance is a goal
Extremes will never do

But something to remember
No matter how we try
We cannot ever balance
The truth with a lie

*

A Prayer for America

May Congress act with conscience
And strive to reach a goal
A decent life for everyone
They play a noble role

May Congress not be blinded
By ideology
Nor play the game of politics
But serve humanity

May love of country guide them
As they reach across the aisle
To make the world a better place
No purpose more worthwhile

May they serve with honor
And cherish every vote
Of those who act with courage
History will take note

*

Ideology

The book of ideology
Echoes like a song
It dictates what to think
Not ponder right or wrong

A symphony of spin resounds
In cadence day by day
With catchy little phrases
That lead the flock astray

Compromise is not in tune
With ideology
Never known to budge an inch
And no apology

It matters not who suffers
Nor who lives or dies
Extreme is quite acceptable
In the ideologue's eyes

Tis time for common sense
To step out on the stage
And sing a song of truth
Tis time to turn the page

*

Corporate America

Corporations are people
The ruling of the day
Along with basic rights
The court had had its say

The masses matter not
In a grand plutocracy
When corporate wealth determines
What will be – will be

Democracy at risk
When one percent holds sway
While ninety nine lose all hope
And dreams fade away

It seems our founders' concept
Of and by and for
Refers to corporations
The people, no more

*

My Flag—My Country

When I see Old Glory
Rippling in the breeze
I marvel at this blessed land
Its mountains, lakes and trees

I think about our founders
Brilliant were they
'Government for people'
O hear these great men say

It is a lofty symbol
That weaves across the land
A symbol of a better life
In freedom's house we stand

May Old Glory bring us honor
As it reaches for the sky
In harmony and peace
On the Fourth of July

*

Ode to
America

Ode to America
(A Cross Country Journey)

From the great Atlantic Ocean
To the Pacific far away
A dream of ours was coming true
To see the USA

A chance to see this blessed land
From sea to shining sea
Its mountains, lakes and prairies
Its breathless scenery

The family car—it was a Ford
With a camper held in tow
This was our home away from home
That summer long ago

We set out with Elisabeth
Our youngest child was she
She'll always be my Betsy
A little girl to me

Beyond the hills of Warren
Our lovely domicile
Beyond New Jersey borders
Lay marvels mile on mile

Before us lay an endless road
That spanned diverse terrain
Captured by New England charm
We reached the coast of Maine

The view was quite spectacular
Where grandeur meets the sea
A gorgeous panorama
Filled our hearts with glee

Behold the many splendid scenes
Found along the way
Snapshots held within my heart
Of a bygone holiday

En route across America
Beyond the towns and malls
A mighty awesome sight appeared
The grand Niagara Falls

Waters roared around us
We sailed The Maid of the Mist
Embraced were we by nature's child
And by its vapor kissed

And then to get another look
From on the other side
We walked across Rainbow Bridge
Enraptured and wide eyed

Great Lakes ever present
Onward we would thrust
Ohio, Indiana
Propelled by wanderlust

Behold the Windy City
Gem of the Middle West
Beautiful Chicago
American treasure chest

The rhythm of the road
Lulled us on our way
Along endless shores
Where rippling waters lay

Farmlands of Wisconsin
A Minnesota fair
Grand Forks, North Dakota
The Plains, so flat, so bare

Miles and miles of nothing
As far as eyes could see
Across the broad horizon
Not a single tree

Mitchell, South Dakota
Corn Palace, USA
On to monumental sights
Mount Rushmore on display

Four icons etched in stone
High above the ground
Stand today in majesty
And evermore resound

America the beautiful
The Rockies brushed the skies
Bubbling springs at Yellowstone
Danced before our eyes

Bison—moose—chipmunks
We hoped to spot a bear
When it appeared in front of us
An answer to a prayer

A great big bear came by our car
Our windows rolled up tight
We got a good long look at him
This filled us with delight

Then off to see Old Faithful
To see her do her thing
She did not disappoint us
Her geyser soon took wing

Filled with awe we traveled on
With yet another sigh
A silhouette of drilling rigs
Toiled against the sky

Idaho and Washington
The Great Northwest at hand
Lumber trucks, floating logs
Scenes that dot the land

We reached the state of Oregon
Where ocean waters swirled
Brilliant seaside vistas
The finest in the world

O Hail the great Pacific
Time to raise a toast
A milestone in our journey
Cheers from coast to coast

Eclectic is a city
Where multi-cultures meet
Hearts in San Francisco sing
To a syncopated beat

Chinatown, Alcatraz
The famous Golden Gate
Fisherman's Wharf and Cable Cars
The street that is not straight

Sequoia Giants—our next stop
Majestic are these kings
Dwarfed we stood encircled by
Earth's oldest living things

The pageantry of tinsel town
Beauty and the beast
Embodiment of fairy tales
Home of pomp and feast

Open roads beckoned us
Time to move along
Eastward, homeward, leeward
Echoing our song

We headed for Las Vegas
In the dead of night
The road ahead was pitch black
And then—a spark of light

At first a tiny twinkle
Then as we neared the town
Twinkles were exploding
And dancing all around

Glitter was its logo
This city with flair
Blinking, pulsing colored lights
Neon everywhere

Moments to remember
We dreamed the night away
By morning we were on the road
Where the blazing desert lay

Our car rolled on in cadence
At last the air turned cool
Another treasure lay in wait
A lofty epic jewel

Once the mighty waters roared
And carved a masterpiece
That echoed through the centuries
Wonders never cease

Canyon walls in splendor
Make the spirit quiver
A winding silver thread below
The Colorado River

Behold the Painted Desert
So different from the East
Brilliant colored ancient rock
Gave our eyes a feast

New Mexico, Texas, Kansas
Dorothy was right
There is no place like home
When it's out of sight

We crossed the Mississippi
Home of Huckleberry Finn
The ghost of Samuel Clemens
Stirred us deep within

New Orleans spawned a classic gift
For the world to share
A gift to stand the test of time
A beat, a soulful prayer

It meant a little more to me
To stand where jazz was born
My father's life was music
His living was his horn

On through Alabama
And then the Sunshine State
Behold the Magic Kingdom
Disney World—how great

This state has much to offer
It has an ocean breeze
Alligator Alley
And the Florida Keys

The Atlantic Ocean greeted us
Then up the coast as planned
To the town—St Augustine
The oldest in the land

The Peach State lay ahead
The Carolinas too
A scent of sweet magnolia
And Smoky Mountain Dew

The National Park like Yellowstone
Except no bubbling springs
Animals and woods and streams
And peaks with smoky rings

We drove up pretty winding roads
Until we had to stop
On foot we climbed to Clingmans Dome
At the very top

A high point in this range
Above six thousand feet
It was worth the effort
Delicious views so sweet

We said goodbye to Smoky
On to the Bluegrass State
Miles of white fenced meadows
And a prancing horse's gait

O Shenandoah Valley
O Washington, DC
Behold our nation's Capitol
It reigns majestically

Up into Philadelphia
And Independence Hall
Echoes of Democracy
Ring for one and all

The red, the white, the blue
Our flag that waves on high
Liberty Bell Pavilion
On the Fourth of July

Let's not forget the people
Americans hand in hand
Twangs and drawls that welcomed us
All across the land

Our romance with the road
Was coming to an end
With visions of America
A panoramic blend

New Jersey is a microcosm
Of the USA
It has the things our country has
But in a smaller way

New Jersey has the mountains
New Jersey has the sea
New Jersey has its share
Of breathless scenery

Our home state so American
And yet there's something more
The greatest city in the world
A jewel right next door

The Big Apple sits there
Underneath our nose
Glowing, bustling, magical
Home of song and prose

Twin towers in magnificence
Embrace a sky of blue
A symbol stands in silhouette
Of lofty dreams come true

At last we reach the Lady
A vision to behold
The Lady holds a gift for us
More precious than gold

She holds the torch of freedom
For the "poor and tempest tossed"
In tribute to the journeys made
And the mighty oceans crossed

"America the beautiful
From sea to shining sea"
O Hail this splendid treasure
Its blessings shine on me

*

INDEX